Dick Wilson, former editor of the Fa
and the China Quarterly, has writ
including seven on China.

Matthew Grenier is a graduate of Manchester University, and
has written articles on contemporary Chinese history for several
Asian periodicals.

DICK WILSON
AND MATTHEW GRENIER

Chinese Communism

SERIES EDITOR
Justin Wintle

Paladin
An Imprint of HarperCollinsPublishers

Paladin
An Imprint of HarperCollins*Publishers*
77–85 Fulham Palace Road,
Hammersmith, London W6 8JB

A Paladin Paperback Original 1992
9 8 7 6 5 4 3 2 1

A catalogue record for this book
is available from the British Library

ISBN 0 586 09024 X

Set in Times

Printed in Great Britain by
HarperCollinsManufacturing Glasgow

Contents

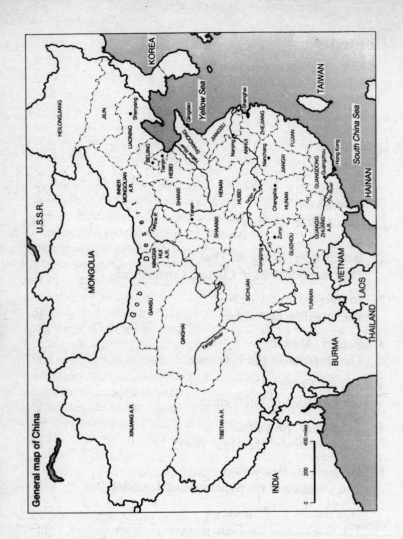

General map of China

Preface

It is the sorrow of modern Chinese intellectuals that after two millennia of recognized superiority, their country's civilization has fallen to such a low point when compared with the flowering of Europe. Dr Joseph Needham, the author of the seven-volume *Science and Civilization in China*, was able to catalogue countless borrowings by European scientists from China in earlier centuries, and the French savants of the eighteenth century openly admired – and copied – the Chinese political system.

In recent times, however, the cultural borrowing has been the other way round as late-imperial and post-imperial China sought desperately to modernize through the use of foreign ideas. The most influential of these, as it turns out, was Communism. The bravado with which Mao Zedong and his colleagues seized power in the 1940s and the refreshing spectacle of their translating Marxism into practical earthy Asian terms caught the imagination, not only of many Chinese who yearned for reform and a fresh start, but also of millions of radicals and young minds in other Asian countries, as well as in Africa, Europe and America, disillusioned with the power politics and shattering economic cycles of international capitalism.

For three eventful decades – the 1950s, 1960s and 1970s – Chinese Communism could claim to be the newest, and most glamorous, ideology circling the world to engage its politically-conscious denizens. Now, lacking the giant figure of Mao, its force seems spent. The Chinese Communist Party seems reduced to fighting old battles and shoring up personal power.

When a communist government turns its weapons on a peaceful popular demonstration in the glare of the world media, another nail is hammered into the coffin of Marxism-Leninism. The massacre of students in Tiananmen Square on 4 June 1989 by the People's Liberation Army highlighted the difficulties which the Chinese Communist leaders have faced continually since the birth of the People's Republic of China in 1949. After over a month of student demonstrations, ignited by the death of the reformist Hu Yaobang and sustained by the arrival of President Gorbachev in Beijing, the divided Chinese leadership looked to the army to reimpose their control over society. What was revealed was not so much a flaw in ideology as a measure of the failure of the system to react to popular discontent, be it in the universities, in the power of local Party cadres, or over the lack of leadership accountability.

The images from China in 1989 were a sad reminder of the universally reactionary nature of one-party states. But to equate Chinese Communism solely with Tiananmen Square would be an historically inaccurate and intellectually unhelpful process. It is the implementation of theory, as the Chinese leaders have discovered in their attempts to apply Marxism-Leninism in China for the past forty years, that led to the contradictions of Tiananmen Square. It is timely, perhaps, to explore precisely what Chinese Communism was, how it appealed to so many Chinese and foreigners, what it stood for and what it accomplished.

Chronology

1957   *On the Correct Handling of Contradictions Among
            the People* written by Mao Zedong
1958   Great Leap Forward
1959   Lushan Plenum sees establishment of two-line
            leadership: Mao Zedong and Liu Shaoqi
1959–62   Three bitter years of crop failure
1960   All Soviet advisers withdrawn from China
1962   Border war against India
1962–4   Liu Shaoqi and Deng Xiaoping promote 'capitalist'
            agricultural policies
1963   Relations with Soviet Communist Party broken
1964   Socialist Education Movement
1966–9   Great Proletarian Cultural Revolution
1969   Sino–Soviet border clashes
1970   Lin Biao, Mao's heir apparent, disappears in
            mysterious circumstances
1971   China admitted to the United Nations
            Nixon visit opens Sino–US rapprochement
1973   Deng Xiaoping rehabilitated after Cultural
            Revolution
1976   Zhou Enlai dies
            Tiananmen Square incident following demonstration
            against Gang of Four
            Deng Xiaoping is dismissed for his role in the
            Tiananmen Square demonstration
            Mao Zedong dies; Hua Guofeng is named as his
            successor
            Gang of Four arrested
1978   Third Plenum marks Deng's endorsement as
            de facto leader
1979   Democracy Wall closed down
            Sino–Vietnamese border clashes
            Open Door policies on foreign investment
1981   Hu Yaobang elected Chairman of Central
            Committee
1984   Sino–British Agreement on the future of Hong
            Kong
1985   'Document No. 1' endorses new enterprise
            agricultural policies

1987   Hu Yaobang ousted from power
1989   Tiananmen Square massacre; 'old guard' block
            reformers
        Zhao Ziyang removed from Chair of Central
            Committee
        Sino–Soviet relations re-established

List of Main Characters

Chen Boda (Ch'en Po-ta) – 1904–89
Joined Communist Party 1927, before studying in Moscow. Worked with Mao Zedong on his *On Practice* and *On Contradictions*, before becoming Mao's personal secretary and principal speech writer. First editor of the Party's theoretical journal, *Red Flag*, 1958. Helped launch of Cultural Revolution with editorial in *People's Daily*, 'Long Live the Thought of Mao Zedong!', 1966. Found guilty of counter-revolutionary activities at Gang of Four trial in 1980. An unpopular aide to the Chairman.

Chen Yun (Ch'en Yun) – 1905–
A print worker who joined the Communist Party in 1925, he worked with Mao in Jiangxi base area, 1929. Long Marcher, sent to Moscow to deliver verdict of famous Zunyi meeting. Vice Premier 1949, distinguished as Communist Party's chief economic theoretician, laying groundwork of centralized economy during 1950s. Opposition to Great Leap Forward led to demotion, re-emerging 1965 as Vice Premier, and very influential after 1978. Left Politburo in 1987, but 'bird-cage' theory still important, and politically aligned with octogenarian conservatives during 1989 demonstrations. Selected works published 1988.

Deng Xiaoping (Teng Hsiao-ping) – 1904–
Joined Communist Party 1924, before studying in France. Elected to Central Committee 1945, Vice Premier 1952, member of Politburo 1955. Removed from Party leadership 1966, returned briefly between 1973 and 1975, before re-emerging as Mao's successor in 1977, when he was reinstated on the Central Committee. Chairman of Military Affairs Commission

and nominal *de facto* leader during most of 1980s. Selected works published 1984. A pragmatic Communist, best known for his, 'It doesn't matter whether the cat is black or white, as long as it catches the mouse.'

Hu Yaobang (Hu Yao-pang) – 1915–89

Joined Youth League 1933, serving under Deng Xiaoping during civil war as political officer. First Secretary of Youth League, 1952. Purged in 1966, re-emerging 1975 as Deng's right-hand man. Elected to Central Committee, 1977, Chairman 1980. Forced to resign as Chairman in 1987 following student pro-democracy demonstrations, but continued working in Central Committee until his death. An impulsive, boyish, iconoclastic man, much admired by intellectuals.

Lin Biao (Lin Piao) – 1908–71

Joined the Communist Party in 1925, and soon commanded his own regiment, showing military brilliance during the Long March and civil war. Politburo member from 1955, Minister of Defence in 1959. Aided Mao's Cultural Revolution through politicization of People's Liberation Army, emerging as Mao's chosen heir. Following attempted coup he was said to have died in a mysterious plane crash while fleeing to the USSR. An embittered megalomaniac who was generally distrusted.

Liu Shaoqi (Liu Shao-ch'i) – 1898–1969

A Hunanese peasant like Mao, Liu joined the Communist Party in 1921, and was active in urban areas before Mao's rise to power in 1935. Vice Chairman of Central People's Government, 1949, Chairman in 1959. Main target of Cultural Revolution, being named as 'China's Khrushchev', and humiliated to his death. Major work, *How to be a Good Communist*. A colourless figure who doubted if collectivization would work in China.

Mao Zedong (Mao Tse-tung) – 1893–1976

Participated in the First Congress of the Chinese Communist Party in 1921. Director of Guomindang's Peasant Department before 1927 split, when he moved to the countryside and led the Autumn Harvest Uprising. Established his leading position in the Party during the Long March, especially after the Zunyi conference in 1935, and thereafter became undisputed leader of the communist movement after Zhang Guotao's challenge to his position failed. Chairman of the Communist Party and leader of China until his death in 1976, although briefly demoted following Great Leap Forward. Five volumes of selected works, and one of selected military writings. He had total faith in the ability of the people to solve their own problems.

Zhao Ziyang (Chao Tzu-yang) – 1919–

Joined Communist Youth League in 1932, but relatively unaffected by civil war. Held important positions in Guangdong, Inner Mongolia and Sichuan provinces after 1949, influencing agricultural policy. Rose to prominence under Deng Xiaoping, being appointed Premier of the People's Republic in 1980. Champion of economic reforms of the 1980s, losing control over policy following his appointment as General Secretary of the Party in 1987. Forced to resign following student demonstrations in 1989. An intellectual who seemed ill at ease in politics.

Zhou Enlai (Chou En-lai) – 1898–1976

Joined Communist Party in 1921 in France before returning as political commissar at the Whampoa Military Academy. He was present at the Shanghai massacre of 1927 and linked with urban revolutionaries before joining Mao in Jiangxi in 1932. After the 1935 Zunyi conference, he was appointed general political director of the Red Army and the Communist Party's public spokesman. After 1949 became the public face of Chinese Communism, as Prime Minister and Foreign Minister, playing the role of the pragmatist over Party policy. Masterminded the Nixon visit in 1972. A man of immense charm and diplomatic skill whose role in the Cultural Revolution is still debated.

1 *Introduction – Eating the Pear –* The Contradictions of Chinese Communism

> The contradiction between imperialism and the Chinese nation and the contradiction between feudalism and the great masses of the people are the basic contradictions in modern Chinese society. Of course, there are others, such as the contradiction between the bourgeoisie and the proletariat and the contradictions within the reactionary ruling classes themselves. But the contradiction between imperialism and the Chinese nation is the principal one.[1]

The 1911 Revolution brought to an abrupt end the dynastic imperial system which had ruled China for two thousand years. China was then plunged into a chaos of internal struggle and external encroachment within an ideological vacuum. The Guomindang, or Nationalist Party, had done most to topple the effete imperial court. But it failed to unite the country ideologically and its authority gradually dissipated under the pressures of warlord separatism, foreign invasion and the growth of a popular movement under the banner of the Chinese Communist Party. When Mao Zedong and his colleagues arrived in triumph in Beijing in 1949 to set up the People's Republic of China, the country was politically divided, economically near-bankrupt and culturally backward, still looking back to the antiquated glories of a past age.

For the people of China, the Communists held out the possibility of both national salvation and social reform. For the Communists themselves, as the quotation from Mao shows, these two goals dictated their philosophical interpretation of a distinctly Western and Eurocentric ideology – Marxism-Leninism. For the more than forty years that they have held power, and the seventy years that they have been in existence, the Chinese Communists have tried to build a socialist system on the foundations of a traditionally feudal authoritarian society. Their theories, encapsulated here in the term 'Chinese Communism', were developed during this struggle to implement Marxism-Leninism within the unpromising actual social conditions in China, particularly in neutralizing the continuing cultural influence of the imperial age.

From the time that the empire was established by the Qin Dynasty in the third century, China had been largely isolated from other early centres of civilization not only by distance, but also by the natural barriers of mountain and desert in the west and the Pacific Ocean in the east. China's vast size and relative isolation were crucial factors in shaping Chinese culture, and in generating a common philosophy and code of conduct among the educated elite, popularly known as Confucianism.

During the Han Dynasty, which followed the Qin, Confucianism was enshrined as the orthodox doctrine of the ruling elite and Confucius was honoured as the great sage and teacher of antiquity. Of all the monarchs who ruled China in the ensuing two magnificent millennia, it was a Manchu emperor, Kang Xi (1661–1722 A.D.) who best exemplified the ideal Confucian ruler. He pushed out the boundaries of the Chinese empire to embrace Korea, Taiwan, Mongolia and Tibet as protectorates, and Confucianism was promoted to become a philosophy of universal application. Kang Xi drafted the famous *Sacred Edict*, which sought to inculcate the Confucian morality among all of his subjects, exalting the twin virtues of filial piety and brotherly love. Confucianism was accepted as the dominant ideology which pervaded every aspect of political, social and family life, and was even institutionalized in the state itself.

At the beginning of the seventeenth century, Matteo Ricci, an Italian Jesuit, initiated officials of the Imperial Court into the laws of natural science which had launched the European renaissance. Many of these ideas were absorbed by intellectuals of the day, but the court itself clung obstinately to 'pure' Confucianism, and when Pope Clement XI unwisely decreed in 1704 that Chinese Christians should denounce Confucianism, their influence on society was negated.

By the time the Western powers arrived in China in the

nineteenth century the Manchu court had fallen into decline. Confucian philosophy had managed to absorb such foreign influences as Buddhism and Taoism, but the economic and military power of the industrialized European countries represented a fearsome new challenge to Chinese society as a whole.

The first response to Western encroachment was the Taiping Rebellion (1848–64), which was inspired by Christian ideals. Its leader, Hung Xiuzhuan, believed he was the Son of God and the younger brother of Jesus Christ, although his rhetoric was firmly rooted in the Confucian tradition. In order to preach the ideal of equality, for instance, he cited a passage in the Confucian treatise, *Evolution of Roles*, dealing with 'cosmopolitanism'. His colleague, Hung Rengan, compared capitalism with the enlightened despotism of another famous Chinese historical figure, the Duke of Chou.

The Taiping were defeated. Then the Self-Strengthening Movement, a band of reformers within the traditional elite, began to implement gradual change and creeping Westernization in Chinese society. At the beginning of the 1890s, however, the Qing Dynasty suffered further blows to its prestige at the hands of foreign powers, especially from the newest 'imperialist', Japan. A new reform movement then started as a nationalistic response to foreign incursions into China, and developed into the first radical attempt to transform the country into a modern nation state. The reformers proposed to work within the existing social and political framework while using Western ideas. Chinese traditional teachings would continue to be the basis for change – 'We must make Chinese learning the foundation.'[2]

Kang Yuwei, one of the leaders of this reform movement, looked to the Confucian classics for inspiration for political reform but questioned the monopolistic interpretative authority of the 'orthodox ancient texts' of Confucian classics. He concluded that Han scholarship was misconceived and the classics written by the Sung scholars were forged. In 1897 he claimed that Confucius had actually created the classics, and not merely edited them as the tradition would have it, invoking antiquity to justify institutional reforms. Revolutionary action against the state could, by implication, be legitimized by the Sage himself.

Kang then went on to derive from the classical sources an evolutionary sequence, which, in its purest form, was reminiscent of Marxist historiography. He theorized that China's evolutionary process was a transition from a period of disorder to a time of peace and partial tranquillity, which in turn would lead to an age of Great Harmony (*Datong*).[3]

Like another of the reformers, Liang Qichao, who wanted to destroy the old Confucian values but not the system itself, Kang Yuwei was not himself a revolutionary. He used Confucius to show that while reform was necessary, it could only be through gradual controlled change. 'Heaven is everlasting,' Kang wrote, 'because it can adapt to change, and so is earth.' By legitimizing the reinterpretation of the Confucian classics, however, Kang opened the floodgates for further theories of what should constitute the new 'heaven on earth'.

The next group of reformers to emerge from the Chinese intellectual elite directly challenged the imperial system itself. The slogan of the China Revolutionary League, founded in Tokyo in 1905, was 'Drive away the Manchus, restore China to the Chinese, establish a republic and equalize landownership.' With the very foundations of the Confucian social system under attack after the 1911 Revolution, Chinese intellectuals looked to Western philosophy for the solution to China's problems – to Kant's dualism, Comte's and Spencer's positivism and Kropotkin's mutual aid theory. The writings of Wang Guowei (1877–1927) reflect the influence of Western dialectical views of history: 'The idealist world outlook is attractive but not credible; the positive method of natural sciences is credible though not attractive.'[4]

The Soviet revolution in Russia in 1917 was hailed by Li Dazhao, one of the first Chinese Marxists, with the words: 'The bell of humanitarianism has rung and the light of freedom has dawned!'[5] Two years later, students and intellectuals across the country demonstrated, in what came to be known as the May 4 Movement, against the parcelling up of Chinese soil into foreign concessions, over the head of the Chinese government, at the Versailles Peace Conference. Mao Zedong later adjudged this an historic occasion. 'The cultural revolution ushered in by the May 4 Movement was a movement for thoroughly opposing feudal culture; since the dawn of Chinese history, there had never been such a great and thoroughgoing cultural revolution.'[6]

In 1921 the Chinese Communist Party was formally established in Shanghai, based on the tenets of Leninism, which shared elements of the Chinese political tradition – the rule of ideologically indoctrinated superior man rather than of laws; the absence of intermediary institutions between state and society; the acceptance of an orthodox, 'correct' view of the world with officials as its moral exemplars exercising power linked to ethical ideas; the intolerance of heterodoxy and political power outside of formal governmental structures; and the perfectibility of man and society through study and self-cultivation.

In his work, *The Awakening of Asia*, Lenin had stated: 'Millions upon millions of people, oppressed and slumbering in medieval stagnancy, have awakened, demand a new life, and struggle for the elementary rights of man, for democracy.'[7] The Chinese Marxist pioneers soon identified which class the success of the Chinese revolution would depend upon. In February 1919, Li Dazhao wrote: 'Our China is a rural nation and a majority of the labouring class is composed of these peasants. If they are not liberated, then our whole nation will not be liberated.'[8]

At the Second Congress of the Chinese Communist Party in 1922, however, the Comintern-imposed manifesto, while acknowledging the importance of the peasantry, assigned it a subordinate role in the revolution. 'Three hundred million Chinese peasants are the most important factors of our revolutionary movement . . . The Chinese revolution will quickly succeed when the majority of the peasants ally with the workers.'[9]

For the following five years, the Communists worked in a united front alliance with the Guomindang or Nationalist Party of Sun Yat-sen and Jiang Jieshi, concentrating on the prospect of urban revolution. When Jiang embarked on his Northern Expedition in 1926, Communist cadres acted as advance propaganda soldiers, ensuring the support of the populace for the revolutionary cause. Their success, however, proved fatal. After a Workers Council had been established in Shanghai, in preparation for the arrival of Nationalist troops, the right wing of the Guomindang, which had its power base in the rural and urban elites, reacted by massacring thousands of Communists and their sympathizers in the city. Throughout 1927, the Communists were attacked by their former allies in urban areas across the south of China. Attempts at urban insurrection by the Communist leadership were consistently crushed.

Mao quickly drew the moral in his celebrated *Report on an Investigation of the Peasant Movement in Hunan* of 1927. 'All talk directed against the peasant movement must be speedily set right,' he insisted. 'All the wrong measures taken by the revolutionary authorities concerning the peasant movement must be speedily changed. Only thus can the future of the revolution be benefited.'[10] The Hunan report is usually presented as the symbolic starting point of Mao's theoretical evolution towards a distinctly Chinese form of Marxism, yet it is replete with Leninist principles. They are evident in Mao's concern with the organization of the peasantry, as well as in his emphasis on the importance of political struggle as the key to economic struggle, which was, according to Lenin, 'the ABC of Marxism'.

In the decade following the failure of the Autumn Harvest Uprising in 1927, Mao was in contact solely with the Chinese peasantry. Attempts by the Communists to apply Leninist organizational structures to a Chinese peasant force under the banner of the proletariat had almost resulted in the annihilation of the entire Party by Jiang Jieshi. The Communists were forced to break out of their southern soviet bases, before embarking on the Long March to a new base in the north. At a conference held in Zunyi during that march, Mao staked his claim to the leadership. His solution to the contradiction between Marxism-Leninism's emphasis on the importance of the proletariat, and the ultimate importance of the peasantry in the Chinese situation, led Mao to call for the Sinification of Marxism.

Mao defined this process in a report to the Central Committee of the Chinese Communist Party in 1938:

What we call concrete Marxism is Marxism that has taken on a national form, that is, Marxism applied to the concrete struggle in the concrete conditions prevailing in China, and not Marxism abstractly used. If a Chinese communist, who is a part of the great Chinese people, bound to his people by his very flesh and blood, talks of Marxism apart from Chinese peculiarities, this Marxism is merely an empty abstraction. Consequently, the Sinification of Marxism – that is to say, making certain that in all of its manifestations it is imbued with Chinese peculiarities, using it according to these peculiarities – becomes a problem that must be understood and solved by the whole party without delay . . . We must put an end to writing eight-legged essays on foreign models . . . We must discard our dogmatism and replace it by a new and vital Chinese style and Chinese manner, pleasing to the eye and to the ear of the Chinese common people.[11]

Marxism-Leninism could serve a useful cause in China only if its 'theories are not . . . looked upon as dogma, but as a guide for action'.[12] In 1942 Mao launched a Rectification Campaign among Party cadres, urging them to take his *On Correcting Mistaken Ideas in the Party*, written in December 1929, as the correct guide for action. At the Seventh Communist Party Congress in 1945, known as the 'Victors' Congress', 'the thought of Mao Zedong' was officially consecrated as the sole guide for the work of the Party. 'The Chinese Communist Party,' the Congress concluded, 'takes the theories of Marxism-Leninism and the unified thought of the practice of the Chinese Revolution, the thought of Mao Zedong, as the guideline of its actions.' Mao claimed for his own works the infallibility he accorded to the theories of Marx and Lenin.

But the next Party Congress, in 1956, saw a wavering in Mao's authority over Party doctrine. 'The Chinese Communist Party takes Marxism-Leninism as the guideline for all of its actions.' Marxism was the guide to the Party's *Weltanschauung*, or world-view. Leninism was the Party's guide on the principles of revolution and organization. Towards the end of the 1950s, however, the dualistic approach of the 1945 Congress was revived, and the ideological role of Leninism was gradually replaced by the thought of Mao Zedong. This dualism suggests that there are two major components of Chinese communist ideology, one being pure (Marxism-Leninism), and the other practical (the thought of Mao Zedong).

The Chinese Communists' view of theory is that Marxism-Leninism is a universal truth which cannot therefore be changed. The word 'Maoism' does not exist in the Party's vocabulary. The word *chuyi*, or -ism, is only attached to a set of ideas characteristic of a class, society or age (landlordism, capitalism, feudalism, socialism). Maoism thus cannot exist as a pure ideology because it is solely an interpretation of Marxism-Leninism. Later, however, by the 1960s, Mao claimed for his own thought the universality he had denied to Marx when calling for the Sinification of Marxism.

An editorial from the *People's Daily* in 1964, at the start of the Socialist Education Movement, indicated how the application of a pure ideology to the concrete conditions existing in China at the time should be achieved:

> The thought of Mao Zedong is one which, in an era moving toward the collapse of imperialism and the victory of socialism, in the great revolutionary struggle of the Chinese people, united the universal truths of Marxism-Leninism with the practice of revolution and construction in China and creatively developed Marxism-Leninism. Our proletarian revolutionary successors must be real Marxist-Leninists and thus must firmly and unflaggingly study the works of Mao Zedong, actively learn and actively use the thought of Mao Zedong.[13]

In 1965, a year before the launching of the Great Proletarian Cultural Revolution, Lin Biao, who was to become Mao's second chosen successor after Liu Shaoqi, made a speech eulogizing the thought of Mao in terms reminiscent of Liu Shaoqi's sycophantic address to the 1945 Congress of Victors. 'The whole series of theories and policies of comrade Mao Zedong concerning people's war,' Lin stated, 'have creatively enriched and developed Marxism-Leninism.'[14] Other references to Mao's 'theories and policies' in Lin's speech can be regarded as an initial attempt to proclaim Mao as the creator not only of a correct practical ideology for the application of Marxism-Leninism in China, but of pure doctrine itself. On 12 August 1966, the Eleventh Plenum of the Central Committee of the Chinese Communist Party actually declared in a communiqué that Mao Zedong Thought was not merely one incarnation of Marxism-Leninism, but a universally applicable guide to Marxism-Leninism.

The thought of Mao Zedong was thus elevated into a position of doctrinal universality, just when Mao's political theories were at their most Sinocentric. For the remainder of his life, Mao's thought was placed in a position of equality with Marxism-Leninism, with Marxism continuing to represent the Chinese Communist world-view, but Mao Zedong Thought replacing Leninism as the guide to organization and revolutionary principles. Since his death, however, the thought of Mao has remained at the heart of Chinese Communist ideology. Although Deng Xiaoping ridiculed both the Cultural Revolutionary Gang of Four and Mao's third chosen successor, Hua Guofeng, for their strict adherence to Mao's thought, labelling them 'whateverists', he still rested his own ideological legitimacy on his interpretation of Mao Zedong Thought.

'Marxism-Leninism-Mao Zedong Thought' continues to be the guiding ideology of the Chinese Communists, and is enshrined in the Party Constitution as one of the pillars of the Four Modernizations (the other three being the socialist road, the dictatorship of the proletariat and the leading role of the Communist Party). From being solely a formula for the practical application of Marxism-Leninism to specific Chinese situations, Mao Zedong Thought has now been elevated into the pure ideology which is verbosely labelled Marxism-Leninism-Mao Zedong Thought. The dualism which began at the 1945 Congress continues to exist. Mao Zedong Thought has merged with Marxism-Leninism into a universal pure ideology, while the present-day policies and actions of the Chinese Communists represent their practical application to the concrete conditions of Chinese society.

To understand why Mao's thought continues to have such a strong influence on Chinese society, it is necessary to examine the philosophical foundations of his works, *On Practice* and *On Contradictions*. These were both written in 1937, a year after the Red Army had reached the haven of Shaanxi province after the ardours of the Long March. They reflect the difficulties that Mao faced in attempting to apply the pure ideology of Marxism-Leninism to the situation in China in the 1930s.

On Practice presents a philosophical justification for Mao's interpretation and implementation of Marxist-Leninist theory along the lines laid down in Marx and Engels' *The Education of the Communist Man*.

> Only through personal participation in the practical struggle to change reality can you uncover the essence of that thing or class of things and comprehend them . . . Knowledge is a matter of science, and no dishonesty or conceit whatsoever is permissible. What is required is definitely the reverse – honesty and modesty. If you want knowledge, you must take part in the practice of changing reality. If you want to know the taste of a pear, you must change the pear by eating it yourself.[15]

The raising of Mao's thought to the level of pure ideology tended, however, to negate the very philosophical basis on which his theory was founded. The strictly doctrinaire approach of the Chinese Communists from 1921 to 1927 had made Mao realize that Marxism-Leninism could be useful only as a theoretical tool. He originally promoted his own thought, therefore, as an example of Marxism-Leninism put into practice. Neither Marx nor Lenin, after all, had had a full opportunity to implement their own theories on the ground.

By the 1960s, however, many of Mao's supporters were going further and claiming universality for his theory. When Hua Guofeng legitimized his leadership position after Mao's death in 1976 through a strictly doctrinaire approach to Mao Zedong Thought, Deng Xiaoping echoed Mao's rebellion against the doctrinaire approach of the 1920s by promoting a more practical ideology. 'You can't just take what Mao Zedong said about one problem,' Deng said in 1978, 'and apply it to some other problem, or take what he said at one place and apply it to some other place, or take what he said at one time and apply it to some other time! . . . There's no such thing as one man being absolutely right.'[16]

Before the historic direction-changing Third Plenum of the Chinese Communist Party in 1978, Hu Yaobang, Deng's choice for Secretary General of the Party, had an article entitled *Practice is the Only Criterion of Truth*, by Hu Fuming, published in the *Guangming Daily*, and on the following day it appeared in the *People's Daily*. The essay stressed that 'whether or not a theory accurately reflects objective reality, whether or not it is true, can only be determined by social practice'.[17] In an attack on the Maoist dogmatists, it stated:

> In theory or in practical work, the Gang of Four set many 'forbidden zones' which fettered people's minds. We must dare to investigate these 'forbidden zones' and dare to correct them because in fact there are no forbidden zones in real science. Whenever there is a 'forbidden zone' which transcends practice and styles itself as absolute, there is no science of real Marxism-Leninism-Mao Zedong Thought; there is only obscurantism, idealism and cultural despotism . . .[18]

Like Mao, Hu Yaobang had also used *On Practice* and *On Contradictions* as his primary intellectual tools. 'If we look at both the positive and negative sides of this problem,' he stated, 'we will learn that Marxism must be constantly enriched and developed in practice. It is not a static, unchanging dogma.' Attacking the 'whatever clique' as empty theorists, Hu continued: 'Those who do not pay attention to learning theory think that practice is theory. They do not understand that though practice can give rise to theory it cannot take the place of theory.' Ultimately, Hu referred back to Lenin to legitimize his theoretical position. Lenin had written:

> Theory must derive its life from practice, must be corrected by practice, must be tested by practice . . . the more ways the better, and the more common experiences there are the richer it will become, and the more reliable, the faster will the

socialist victory be achieved, and the more easily will practice create – because only practice can create – the best ways and means of struggle.[19]

The problem for the Chinese Communists today mirrors that of modern interpreters of Confucius, namely to distinguish between what Mao actually said and the inherited 'correct' framework of Mao Zedong Thought. Without Marxism-Leninism, Mao Zedong would appear as just another successful nationalist. With Marxism-Leninism, however, Mao's mistakes are not just mistakes, but part of the dialectical process of history. Mao Zedong Thought may have been placed on the same level as Marxism-Leninism in the Four Modernizations, but in essence it has been demoted, as no longer representing a practical ideology for the concrete conditions which exist in China.

Rather, the Dengist emphasis on practice enables Party leaders to legitimize a continuation of Communist Party rule, through the use of those parts of Mao Zedong Thought which serve the practical ideology of the Communist Party. When Su Shaozhi, the head of the Institute for Marxism-Leninism-Mao Zedong Thought, stated that Marxism-Leninism was scientific because it was willing to change its theories in the light of new evidence, however, he was accused of the 'heresy of revisionism'.[20] Practice, while being the 'sole criterion of the truth', will never become the final arbiter of ideology. This control still rests firmly in the hands of the Party leadership.

Mao's other major philosophical contribution to Chinese Communist ideology was the second of the pair of essays to which *On Practice* belongs – *On Contradictions*. Mao wrote:

The law of contradiction in things, that is, the law of the unity of opposites, is the fundamental law of nature and of society and therefore also the fundamental law of thought . . . According to dialectical materialism, contradiction is present in all processes of objectively existing things and of subjective thought and permeates all these processes from beginning to end; this is the universality and absoluteness of contradiction.[21]

For Mao, there were two forms of contradiction – one between the enemy and the people, and the other 'among the people'. The first was antagonistic, and the law of the unity of opposites did not apply because the enemy would be destroyed and unity would be created among the people. The second was non-antagonistic, and could be resolved through the peaceful means of criticism and self-criticism. All previous popular rebellions in Chinese history had failed, Mao argued, because of their inability to distinguish between their real friends and their real enemies. The law of contradictions would aid the Chinese Communists' victory, therefore, by identifying their major enemies via an analysis of the principal and secondary contradictions existing in society at any given moment.

The idea that contradictions are universal and a motor of change had originally been stated by Hegel, was developed by Engels in his *Dialectics of Nature*, and was then extensively used by Lenin. To Mao in 1937, however, the importance of contradictions in society could not be over-emphasized. 'Everywhere in the world there are contradictions. If there were no contradictions there would be no world.'[22] Mao regarded contradictions as having practical functions, called the 'law of the unity of opposites', and this is the most important specific theory which the practical ideology of Mao Zedong Thought took from the general body of the pure Marxist-Leninist theory.

Mao criticized Engels' three great and coequal laws of dialectical materialism. 'Of Engels' three categories,' Mao argued, 'I do not believe that two, the mutual transformation of qualitative and quantitative change and the negation of a negation, are on the same level as the unity of opposites. This is a three-part pluralism, not monism. The most fundamental is the unity of opposites.'[23] In other words, Mao made the unity of opposites in a contradiction into the only fundamental law of dialectics (one always divides into two), but rejected the three stages of dialectical development – 'thesis, antithesis, and synthesis'.

In 1963, Yang Xianzhen attacked Mao's 'one into two' theory, by stating that 'two combine into one'. In a published lecture at one of the rotating training classes of the Party School, Yang asked, 'What does one affirmation of one affirmation, one negation of one negation, one affirmation of one negation, and one negation of one affirmation mean?' Mao responded by saying, 'Yang Xianzhen has suggested that two combines into one, by which he means that two different things are inseparably tied together. Where in the world is there any tie that cannot be cut? There may be a relationship, but it must always be cut. There is nothing that cannot be divided.'[24]

Some Soviet and Chinese philosophers felt that Mao's understanding of contradictions was inspired not so much by Marxist dialectics but by the old traditional Chinese dialectic of waxing and waning, decline and renewal, the *yin* and the *yang*. In Mao's *Talks on Questions of Philosophy*, in 1964, he stated:

> Affirmation, negation, affirmation, negation . . . in the development of things, every link in the chain of events is both affirmation and negation. Slave-holding societies negated primitive society, but with reference to feudal society it constituted, in turn, the affirmation. Feudal society constituted the negation in relation to slave-holding society but it was in turn the affirmation with reference to capitalist society. Capitalist society was the negation in relation to feudal society, but it is, in turn, the affirmation in relation to socialist society.[25]

Mao therefore utterly rejected the principle of the negation of the negation as an axiom of dialectics, on the grounds that every historical phenomenon was simultaneously or successively affirmation or negation. This does indicate a certain affinity with the traditional Chinese view of history as flux and reflux, rather than as a purposeful Marxian forward movement. By dividing every contradiction, however, the situation is never static, because 'the principal and the non-principal aspects of a contradiction transform themselves into each other and the nature of things changes accordingly'.[26] This enabled the Chinese leaders to inject an element of realism and flexibility into the decision-making process, while retaining the inevitability of the Marxian progress towards a communist society.

Hu Yaobang, while faithful to Engels' theory of dialectical materialism, echoed Mao's affinity with traditional Chinese historiography. 'From disunity and inconsistency, in the process of practice, through discussion, knowledge becomes continually deeper, more unified, more consistent, moving forward to disunity again, and yet again to inconsistency. It is the cyclical nature of this process that gradually raises knowledge to a new and higher level.'[27] Hu was critical of Mao because his emphasis on contradictions in a socialist society had resulted in them being 'treated as contradictions between us and the enemy'.[28]

Mao's fundamental law of dialectics, that one can always be divided into two, led him to argue that reactionary and erroneous tendencies constantly emerge not only within a post-revolutionary society as a whole, but also within the Communist Party itself. He concluded that the only way to combat such tendencies was through a continuous process of class struggle. Indeed, for Mao, contradictions were not merely a motor of change, as they were for Marx and Hegel, but the very engine of life and reality. 'If there were no contradictions and no struggle,' he stated in 1958, 'there would be no world, no progress, no life, there would be nothing at all.'[29]

In the 1958 Party Congress, Liu Shaoqi had rehabilitated the term originally used by Trotsky, but which Mao now applied as a basic philosophical tool for the Chinese Communists – that of permanent revolution. Mao announced in the same year:

> I stand for the theory of permanent revolution. Do not mistake this for Trotsky's theory of permanent revolution. In making revolution one must strike while the iron is hot – one revolution must follow another, the revolution must continually advance. The Hunanese often say, 'Straw sandals have no pattern – they shape themselves in the making.'[30]

The *People's Daily* editorial of August 1964 quoted earlier also provides a doctrinal formulation of Marxism-Leninism and Mao Zedong Thought:

> The spirit of Marxism-Leninism in its philosophical-ideological aspects is dialectical materialism, especially the law of the unity of opposites. In its political-ideological aspects, it is the theory of class struggle, especially the theory of

proletarian revolution and proletarian dictatorship. Real
Marxist-Leninists must use the law of the unity of opposites
to resolve problems, must always uphold the proletarian
revolution and the proletarian dictatorship.[31]

Mao's first philosophical essay, *On Practice*, was invoked by
his successors to legitimize the continued rule of the Communist
Party. In the case of the second essay, *On Contradictions*,
however, contemporary leaders face a contradiction of their
own. By accepting Mao Zedong Thought as a theoretical tool,
they concede a belief in the use of the law of the unity of
opposites, and thus in the continued need for class struggle.
However, most of the leaders were painfully and personally
affected by the logical outcome of Mao's theory of permanent
revolution – the Cultural Revolution.

In 1980, therefore, the Party announced (as it had also done in
1956) that classes had been eliminated from society. There was
to be no more emphasis on class struggle. Instead, reform was to
become the new, and most dynamic, motor of change. 'Socialist
society is a society that advances through reform,' Zhao Ziyang
stated. 'Reform is a process by which the socialist relations of
production and the socialist superstructure improve themselves
and it is also a force that pushes all work forward.'[32]

Just as the Eighth Party Congress had aimed for a gradual
road to socialism, so the reform leadership pointed out that
Mao's vision of socialism overnight would not be possible.

China is now in the primary stage of socialism. But precisely
because our socialism has emerged from the womb of a
semi-colonial, semi-feudal society, with the productive forces
lagging behind those of the developed capitalist countries,
we are destined to go through a very long primary stage.
During this stage we shall accomplish industrialization and
the commercialization, socialization and modernization of
production, which many other countries have achieved under
capitalist conditions.[33]

In trying to turn the clock back to the 'golden years' of
the early 1950s, however, the Chinese Communists are still

hampered by the three decades of political struggle, within society and the Party, that came between. On the eve of the Cultural Revolution, Mao stated:

> Basing themselves on the changes in the Soviet Union, the imperialist prophets are pinning their hopes of 'peaceful evolution' on the third or fourth generation of the Chinese Party. We must shatter these imperialist prophecies. From our highest organization down to the grass-roots, we must everywhere give constant attention to the training and upbringing of successors to the revolutionary cause.[34]

Although the 1980s have seen the replacement of '-isms' with 'izes' – from socialism, capitalism, revisionism and imperialism to modernization, commercialization and decentralization – the importance of political struggle has continued. A 1981 Party Resolution shows the weight still placed on this. 'Class struggle will continue to exist within certain limits for a long time to come and may even grow acute under certain conditions.'[35]

After the 1989 Tiananmen Square massacre, the Party once more acted according to Maoist principles. Its new Secretary General, Jiang Zemin, elaborated, in his National Day 1989 speech, what the State Council spokesman described as 'the political manifesto of China's third-generation collective leadership'. First, doctrines of working-class leadership and the importance of the worker–peasant alliance were revived. A distinction was made between 'two kinds of reform and opening' as a prelude to scaling down the reform and opening policies of the 1980s. Third, the absolute superiority of socialism and the ultimate infallibility of the Chinese Communist Party were reasserted. Fourth, an international environment was depicted in which China is besieged by hostile reactionary forces.[36]

The contradictions which caused Mao first to reappraise Marxism-Leninism and eventually to promote his own theory are a major strand in the development of Chinese Communism. Just as the reformers of the 1890s had been forced to reappraise Confucianism in order to continue in power, so the Chinese Communists have constantly been hampered by the contradictions that exist between Marxism-Leninism and the actual political, economic and cultural conditions of Chinese society. The question is not whether the theory that has emerged is more Chinese or more Marxist, but rather how the Chinese Communists have had ceaselessly to adapt themselves to new situations and new conditions in applying Marxism-Leninism to Chinese society. These can be summed up in the principal contradictions between democracy and centralism, between economic planning and the market, and between the red or expert individual roles in social change.

In 1962, Mao made his clearest assessment of the philosophy of Marxism-Leninism-Mao Zedong Thought:

> Socialist society covers a very long historical period. Classes and class struggle continue to exist in this society and the struggle still goes on between the road of socialism and the road of capitalism. The socialist revolution on the economic front (in the ownership of the means of production) is insufficient itself and cannot be consolidated. There must be a thorough socialist revolution on the political and ideological fronts. Here a very long period of time is needed to decide 'who will win' in the struggle between socialism and capitalism. Several decades won't do it; success requires anywhere from one to several centuries.[37]

Such was the magisterial time-scale in which Mao required his followers to work.

2 *Democracy vs. Centralism* – The Question of Politics

During Mao's student days in Changsha, there was an uprising against the Qing Dynasty officials in the town who preferred to let people starve, rather than open the local government food stores to them. The leaders of the revolt were branded as rebels and beheaded. In an interview with Edgar Snow in 1936, Mao recalled the event:

> This incident was discussed in my school for many days. It made a deep impression on me. Most of the other students sympathized with the 'insurrectionists', but only from an observer's point of view. They did not understand that it had any relation to their own lives . . . I never forgot it. I felt that there with the rebels were ordinary people like my own family and I deeply resented the injustice of the treatment given to them.[1]

To understand the Communist Party's position within Chinese society, both before and after the revolution, it is as well to bear in mind the peasant background of most of its leaders, and also the tradition of peasant protest against unjust rulers which Mao had witnessed in Changsha. In the 1920s, the peasantry accounted for 80 per cent of China's population and suffered just as much as the nascent urban proletariat from the effects of the unequal treaties imposed by the imperialist powers. From its inception, the Chinese Communist Party was divided between the rural and urban constituents of the political situation. Chen Duxiu, one of the founders of the Communist Party, pursued policies which were oriented towards the urban proletariat in the classic Marxist tradition, whereas Peng Pai, Mao's predecessor as Director of the Peasant Movement Training

Institute, concentrated on the quite different challenges of the countryside.

In his report to the Third Party Congress in Guangzhou in 1923, Chen Duxiu did not even mention Peng's work with the peasantry. Instead, he lamented the fact that although the peasantry were numerous, they were backward and impossible to motivate. Maring, the Comintern representative, 'had always held the peasants in contempt, and he did not mention a word about the peasant problem', a reproachful Chinese comrade observed. Yet the manifesto finally adopted by the Party, backed by the full weight of the Comintern, accepted the leadership of the Guomindang in the national revolution. The peasantry were apparently irrelevant to the success of the revolution.[2]

For the next four years, the Chinese Communists worked within this limited framework of the united front with the Guomindang. The early success of the Northern Expedition, which aimed to unite China under the banner of Sun Yat-sen's three principles (nationalism, democracy and the people's livelihood), heavily depended on the advance propaganda work of Communist Party cadres in both rural and urban areas. Even before the massacre of Communist cadres and their supporters in Shanghai in 1927, however, the united front was beginning to show signs of collapse. Jiang Jieshi, whose strength rested upon the national bourgeoisie and the continuation of trade with the Western powers, was determined to eliminate Communist influence in the cities. Shanghai was the showpiece of foreign capitalism at work in China, and the strength of its workers' movement posed a challenge to Jiang.

Although the Shanghai massacre was a severe blow to the Communists, it did not dampen the Party's enthusiasm for a working-class-based revolution. Throughout 1927, the Communists attempted to rekindle the flame of urban revolution which Jiang's actions had doused, by starting uprisings in the southern cities of China. In Nanchang, Changsha and Guangzhou, the Communists, still half-hidden behind the banner of a united Guomindang–Communist alliance, were singularly unsuccessful. The fledgling Red Army, which the Nanchang uprising produced, was forced to march across the country in search of new power bases and popular support.[3]

Mao's famous *Report on an Investigation of the Peasant Movement in Hunan*, concluded that the locus of revolution was now moving away from the cities to the countryside.

Within a very short time, several hundred million peasants from the provinces of China's central, southern and northern sections will rise up, and their power will be like a blasting wind and cloudburst so extraordinarily swift and violent that no force however large will be able to suppress it. They will burst through all trammels that restrain them, and rush toward the road of liberation.[4]

Mao did not deny the working class a significant role in China's revolution:

The industrial proletariat is the most progressive class in modern China and has become the leading force in the revolutionary movement . . . They have been deprived of all means of production, have nothing left but their hands, have no hope of ever becoming rich and, moreover, are subjected to the most ruthless treatment by the imperialists, the warlords and the bourgeoisie. That is why they are particularly good fighters.[5]

But the failure of the Party since 1921, Mao suggested, had been its reliance on the urban areas as the only possible source of popular support for the revolutionary cause. 'Every revolutionary comrade should know that the national revolution requires a profound change in the countryside. The revolution of 1911 did not bring about this change, hence its failure.'[6]

Following the failure of the Autumn Harvest Uprising in Changsha in 1927, Mao was accused by his Party colleagues of military opportunism, inadequate peasant mobilization, collaboration with bandits and failure to obey Party Central Committee directives. He was dismissed from his alternate membership of the Politburo. Yet he persevered with the peasantry, establishing a soviet base with the help of Zhu De, later to become the most senior of China's military leaders, on the borders of Hunan and Jiangxi provinces. Mao began formulating policies based on the strength of the peasantry. He argued that by forming rural soviets with the backing of the local inhabitants, the Party would be able gradually to extend the area under their control in a series of waves, until they were strong enough to launch an attack on Guomindang-held towns and cities. Here was the beginning of Mao's reversal of Marxist theory, with the countryside playing the dominant role in the revolution.

In April 1929, in a report to the Central Committee, Mao answered his critics within the Party who claimed he was ignoring Marxist principles about the importance of the proletariat. It was a mistake, he wrote,

> to fear the development of the power of the peasants lest it overtake the leadership of the workers and hence become detrimental to the revolution. For the revolution in semi-colonial China will fail only if the peasant struggle is deprived of the leadership of the workers; it will never suffer just because the peasant struggle develops in such a way that the peasants become more powerful than the workers.[7]

The Comintern-dominated Party leadership was unimpressed. Li Lisan, the new Secretary General, advocated from his underground headquarters in Shanghai a new putschist policy, believing that the time was ripe for the Red Army to seize urban areas, thus supplying the necessary proletarian hegemony for the anticipated agrarian revolt. In a letter to Lin Biao in 1930, entitled *A Single Spark Can Start a Prairie Fire*, Mao tried to reconcile his views with those of the Party centre.

> The laying of the Party's proletarian basis and the establishment of the Party branches in industrial enterprises in key districts are the important organizational tasks of the Party at present; but at the same time the development of struggles in the countryside, the establishment of the Red political power in small areas, and the creation and expansion of the Red Army, are in particular the main conditions for helping the struggle in the cities and accelerating the revolutionary upsurge.[8]

Li Lisan's policy, as Mao had warned, was a fiasco. The Red Army was defeated in Changsha because of lack of support from the urban workers, and Jiang Jieshi once more turned his guns upon the Communists. By 1934, the urban-oriented Party leaders had all been driven to the rural bases, but Mao had to wait until the Zunyi conference in 1935 to stake his claim as leader of the Communist Party. By the time the remnants of the Red Army completed their Long March to Shaanxi province, in northern China, Mao's claim was apparently secure. His views on the importance of the peasantry and the countryside in the Chinese revolution had remained unchanged since the mid-1920s and were proved correct. After the signing of another united front agreement with the Guomindang, this time against the Japanese in 1937, Mao was at last able to try to formulate these policies within a sufficiently rigorous Marxist framework.

In his *The Chinese Revolution and the Chinese Communist Party*, written in 1939, Mao identified the outstanding qualities which made the Chinese proletariat 'the basic motive force of the Chinese revolution' – first, because it was subjected to a threefold oppression (imperialist, bourgeois and feudal); second, because it was under the leadership of the Communist Party, and was thus the most politically-conscious class in Chinese society; and, third, 'because the Chinese proletariat by origin is largely made up of bankrupted peasants, it has natural ties with the peasant masses'. Therefore, 'Unless it is led by the proletariat,' Mao concluded, 'the Chinese revolution cannot possibly succeed.' But the peasantry were 'the natural and most reliable ally of the proletariat and the main contingent of China's revolutionary forces'.[9]

In Mao's *On New Democracy*, he argued that after the May 4 Movement in 1919, the 'political leader of China's bourgeois-democratic revolution was no longer the bourgeoisie but the proletariat'.[10] However, as Lenin had argued, it would be necessary for the working class to form alliances with other classes, especially the peasantry, during the democratic, or pre-socialist, period of revolution.

Although Lenin himself had not been in favour of allying with the national bourgeoisie, Mao argued that because China was a semi-colonial country which had been the victim of aggression, 'the task of the proletariat is to form a united front with the national bourgeoisie against imperialism and the bureaucrat and warlord governments without overlooking its revolutionary quality'.[11] In the civil war era, moreover, the Communist Party was appealing not just to the peasantry, but also to the urban intellectual and social elites, who were disaffected with the Guomindang government but worried about the spectre of a radical Communist Party taking its place.

In his *On New Democracy* in 1940, one of his most seminal writings, Mao stated that 'the progress of the Chinese Revolution must be divided into two stages: (1) the democratic revolution; (2) the socialist revolution . . . The above-mentioned democracy does not have the meaning of the old democracy, but is a new type of democracy, or new democracy.'[12]

On the eve of the Communist Party's victory in 1949, Mao expanded these theories in his work, *On the People's Democratic Dictatorship*. Its ideas can be traced back to Lenin's *Democratic Dictatorship of Workers and Peasants* in which the Russian revolutionary showed that such a state was democratic because it was directed against the reactionary classes. Lenin, however, had never been obliged to answer the question of how a dictatorship – a government enforcing a single uniform policy – can be based on a coalition of parties, each based on differing class interests.

Mao's answer was that the working class were 'the leaders of the revolution and have the highest revolutionary spirit', and because the Communist Party was the voice of the working class, it would assume a dominant position within the government.[13] In *On New Democracy*, Mao defined the state form as 'the joint dictatorship of several revolutionary classes', and the governmental form as 'democratic centralism'.[14] By 1949 he shifted the emphasis from democracy to the dictatorship of the proletariat: 'A state system which is shared only by the common people and which the bourgeoisie is not allowed to own privately; add to this the leadership of the working class, and we have the state system of one people's democratic dictatorship.'[15]

At the second session of the Seventh Plenum of the Central Committee of the Communist Party in March 1949, it was announced who else was to be included in the joint dictatorship:

> The people's democratic dictatorship led by the proletariat and based on the worker–peasant alliance, requires that our party conscientiously unite with the entire working class, the entire peasantry and the broad masses of revolutionary intellectuals; these are the leading and basic forces of the dictatorship . . . It is also required that our party unite with as many as possible of the representatives of the urban petty bourgeoisie and national bourgeoisie who can co-operate with us, and with their intellectuals and political groups.[16]

This class nature of the state and its sphere of authority has been elegantly defined by Stuart Schram as a 'concentric circle metaphor'.[17] Mao used Stalin's four-class bloc to explain the representatives of the joint dictatorship – the working class, which was the leading revolutionary party commanding most authority; the peasantry, which would be its most reliable ally; the petty bourgeoisie, which consisted mostly of followers; and the national or liberal bourgeoisie which played a dual role, as part of the people and thus represented in the people's government, but also as exploiters, and, therefore, counter-revolutionaries. Thus, if individuals in the national bourgeoisie behaved according to the rules of the government, they were part of the people. If not, they were reactionaries to be execrated.

In this way, Mao was able to embrace middle-class Chinese who were useful to Chinese society, while maintaining the façade of a united front of all revolutionary groups. The working class was at the middle of this circle of unity, with all power emanating from it – or rather its representative, the Communist Party. Once individuals or groups strayed outside the circle, they were going against the wishes of the 'democratic centre', or the majority of the people, and were therefore punishable.

Lenin had defined democratic centralism in terms of organizational principles: the Party should have freedom of discussion, but adhere to decisions once they had been adopted; the leaders should consult with the rank and file, but thereafter there should be absolute obedience of lower organs to higher organs. Lenin's democratic centralism defines the correct functioning of the Communist Party itself, though the same principles were supposed to apply to such other political and economic organizations as trade unions and the bureaucracy. Mao also used the term in discussing the Communist Party, but employed it more broadly to characterize the spirit of Chinese society as a whole, and the relationship between leadership and led. 'This difference in usage,' Schram concludes, 'stands . . . as a symbol of the crucial difference between Mao Zedong's thought and orthodox Leninism.'[18]

Mao had laid down his initial laws concerning democratic centralism in an article, *On Correcting Mistaken Ideas in the Party*, written in December 1929.

> In the sphere of organization, ensure democracy under centralized guidance. It should be done on the following lines:
> (1) The leading bodies of the Party must give a correct line of guidance and find solutions when problems arise, in order to establish themselves as centres of leadership.
> (2) The higher bodies must be familiar with the life of the masses . . . so as to have an objective basis for correct guidance.
> (3) No Party organization at any level should make any casual decisions in solving problems. Once a decision is reached, it must be firmly carried out.
> (4) All decisions of any importance made by the Party's higher bodies must be promptly transmitted to the lower bodies and the Party rank and file . . .
> (5) The lower bodies of the Party and the Party rank and file must discuss the higher bodies' directives in order to understand their meaning thoroughly and decide on the methods of carrying them out.[19]

Again, in 1942, when attempting to unite the leadership behind his views, Mao stressed the importance of centralism. 'The Communist Party not only needs democracy, but needs centralization even more.'[20]

After the Communists' victory in the civil war in 1949, they returned triumphantly to the cities which had almost been the scene of their destruction twenty-two years earlier. In March, Mao stated that 'The period of "from the city to the village" and of the city leading the village has now begun. The centre of gravity of the Party's work has shifted from the village to the city.'[21] The Communists established a People's Political Consultative Conference to finalize the decisions already taken within the Party, as a symbol of their intention to promote a democratic and united front. It issued an Organic Law of the Central People's Government, the principal embodiment of which was a united front of all democratic organizations. These non-Communist political parties have continued to exist, powerless, throughout the history of the People's Republic.

While promoting a façade of democracy, the Communists in the urban areas were led by the lack of material support to emphasize the importance of organization, and adherence of state bureaucrats to the Party line. In June 1949, All-China Associations of Cultural Workers were formed, followed by the All-China Federation of Labour, with the aim of uniting as many people as possible behind the new government.[22] As Franz Schurmann has noted, 'When a revolution destroys a social system, it also annihilates its elites. The new revolutionary regime can only pull society together again through organization. Political centralization is one of the forms that post-revolutionary organization has taken.'[23]

According to Liu Shaoqi, speaking in Yan'an in 1941, the Chinese Communists had the advantage of taking the Communist Party of the Soviet Union as their living example: 'The majority of our Party members can recite from memory the organizational principles of the Bolshevik Party.'[24] Throughout China after the revolution, Party organizations were established to mirror state bureaucracies along Leninist lines, and during the initial stages of the People's Republic, administrators were left relatively untouched by the Party's emphasis on class struggle. The Communists pragmatically realized that without the tentative support of the bureaucrats, they would be unable to implement their policies.

Mao Zedong was concerned, however, lest the Party would,

by working within a vertically stratifying organizational structure, become divorced from the people that it claimed to represent. During the Yan'an era (1937–45), the efficiency of organization had been lower in Yan'an itself than in the front-line bases, because of the excessive bureaucratism of Party cadres, who were inhibited from criticizing anything which appeared to have the authority of the Central Committee behind it. In 1943, in his *Concerning the Methods of Leadership*, Mao criticized cadres whose 'leadership becomes bureaucratic and divorced from the masses'. Correct leadership of the Party, in all its practical work, should be 'from the masses, to the masses'.

> This means: take the ideas of the masses (scattered and unsystematic ideas) and concentrate them (through study, turn them into concentrated and systematic ideas), then go to the masses and propagate and explain these ideas until the masses embrace them as their own, hold fast to them and translate them into action, and test the correctness of these ideas in such action. Then once again concentrate ideas from the masses and once again go to the masses so that the ideas are persevered in and carried through. And so on, over and over again in an endless spiral, with the ideas becoming more correct, more vital and richer each time. Such is the Marxist theory of knowledge.[25]

Mao here was beginning to divide the orthodox Marxist-Leninist view of Party organizational policy (democratic centralism) into two distinct, and contradictory, entities – democracy in the form of the mass-line, and centralism in the form of the importance of organization. At the Eighth Party Congress in 1956, class struggle was downgraded in the list of priorities and greater stress given to democracy. This was an apparent resolution of this principal contradiction between centralism and democracy, and between the centre and the regions, leading to the 'downward transfer of authority' to the regional level. During the Great Leap Forward that followed, the Party pursued the centralization of general policy impulses and decentralization of specific policy impulses, encapsulated in the slogan 'Centralized Policy and Divided Management'.

Part of the reason for this was the tendency during the First Five Year Plan for the six regions of China, which had been temporarily established after 1949, to develop vested interests, acting against the goals of the centre. This had especially been the case in the north-east of the country, where Gao Gang was removed as leader in 1954 after a special investigation team headed by Deng Xiaoping had accused him of attempting to set up an independent kingdom. Thus the Party centre tried to use regionalism to fight regionalism. In February 1957, Mao summed up this approach: 'The unity of this kind of democracy and centralism, the unity of freedom and discipline – this is our system of democratic centralism.'[26]

In May of the same year, the democracy of the One Hundred Flowers Movement was denounced by the Party as petit bourgeois and counter-revolutionary. However, Mao intoned a new kind of freedom theme – the creativity and initiative of the masses, similar to the spontaneous populist upsurge of the masses which the Russians since Lenin had consistently denounced. Mao aimed to liberate the masses by removing those restraints which prevented them from releasing energy and impulses necessary for the Party's correct leadership. Centralism would be used to channel and direct these impulses, thus realizing the unity of the contradiction between centralism and democracy.

The Party's role would be to promote this element of radicalism in society, as a counterweight to the element of conservatism inherent in vertically stratified bureaucracy. This, in turn, led to Mao's formulation in 1957, which was written finally into the Party Constitution in 1969: 'We must bring about a political climate which has both centralism and democracy, discipline and freedom, unity of purpose and ease of mind for the individual, and which is lively and vigorous.'[27]

At the beginning of the One Hundred Flowers Movement, Mao had stated that 'democracy is both an ends and a means', but by June 1957, as we have seen, his views had changed. 'Democracy as such sometimes seems to be an end,' he wrote, 'but it is in fact only a means.'[28] The establishment of people's communes during the Great Leap Forward was meant to provide the Party with the political framework necessary for releasing the energy and initiative of the masses which would serve the Communists' ultimate aim – a socialist society.

One of the problems of the Great Leap, however, was that the authority of the Party centre was so strong in providing the impetus for the communization programme that Party cadres at the grass roots were unable to refine the general policy to suit local conditions. Output targets set by the authorities in Beijing were inflated first at provincial level and then again at county level, before the local cadres had even had the chance to assess whether the original figures were realistic. To doubt the chances of fulfilling these targets after they had been set by higher political authorities called for superhuman courage, so it was virtually impossible for any democratic impulses to reach the Party centre. The shortfalls of the Great Leap Forward, which were prolonged because of adverse weather conditions, were largely a result of these idealistic speeches and 'hoped-for' output figures on the part of the Party leadership.

With Mao's self-removal from the substantive policy-making process after 1959, the Party leadership once again became more centralized. But Mao continued to promote the contradiction between democracy and centralism as the principal contradiction that the Party should struggle against. In a speech at the '7,000 Cadres Conference' in 1962, he stated: 'Without democracy, there cannot be any correct centralism because people's ideas differ, and if their understanding of things lacks unity then centralism cannot be established. What is centralism? First of all it is a centralization of correct ideas . . .'[29] This acknowledges the need for information to flow from the grass roots to the otherwise starved centre, but simultaneously implies that only if people are consulted will they subsequently be in the right frame of mind to accept the decisions of leading organs.

In 1942 Mao had led a Rectification, or *Zhengfeng*, campaign within the Party in its Yan'an base to consolidate both his position and his theoretical views within the Party. In 1956, he went outside the Party to recruit the intellectuals in his war against wrong ideas in the Party, declaring that classes were a thing of the past and that class struggle would no longer be necessary. By 1962, however, Mao was still struggling with the unresolved contradiction about the Party's role in the post-revolutionary society. His attempts to provoke discussion about the role of the Party in China during the One Hundred Flowers Movement floundered because most of the intellectuals who 'bloomed' did not agree that China should necessarily be following the socialist road, as prescribed by the Communist Party. The next logical step in this process of attempting to maintain the Party's role as the proletarian standard bearer of the revolution, after using the Party against the Party, and then the intellectuals against the Party, was to turn to the masses themselves.

In his speech *On the Correct Handling of Contradictions Among the People* in 1957, Mao had stated that, 'Our People's Government is one that genuinely represents the people's interests, it is a government that serves the people. Nevertheless, there are still certain contradictions between this government and the people.'[30] This implied that there could also be a contradiction between the Party and the people – an admission akin to a Hegelian negation of a negation, because the Party's legitimacy was based, after all, on the belief that it was the true expression of the people.

During the 1960s Western Marxists argued that alienation could continue to exist in a socialist society, and although Zhou Yang vehemently attacked this viewpoint in 1963, it is a very similar argument to the theories which led Mao in 1966 to launch the Great Proletarian Cultural Revolution in which he urged the masses to attack Party cadres for their mistakes. Wang Ruoshui, who later became a prime target of the spiritual pollution campaign in 1983, used the alienation theory to show how the Communists could abandon their intended role as servants of the people and become their masters instead.

In 1981, Wang argued in his *On Alienation* that:

Once a Party which was formerly under oppression comes in to power, its position is changed. There is the danger that it will cut itself off from the masses and become alienated; there is the possibility for it to become alienated . . . This possibility exists at all levels of our leadership and has not yet been solved. The Party Central Committee has taken notice of it. Promoting democracy, perfecting the legal system, laying down the rules governing life in our Party, and abolishing the system of life-long appointment of cadres – we may say these are all measures for preventing alienation.[31]

Mao believed not only that the Party had become cut off from the masses, but also that its conservative tendencies would enable capitalism to re-establish itself in China. Mao's answer, unlike Wang's, lay in freeing the masses of their servile attitude towards authority of any kind, whether against intellectuals, bureaucrats or ultimately Party cadres and leaders themselves. Wang argued instead that capitalism could not be 'brought back' by these people within the Party, because it had never sufficiently established itself in the first place. Rather, he argued, there was a natural tendency for the Communists, when promoting the centralism side of the contradiction, to turn to traditional feudal forms of authoritarian rule.

The Sixteen Point Decision on the Cultural Revolution, of August 1966, stated that the new Cultural Revolution groups should be established by 'a system of general elections, like that of the Paris Commune . . .' Once elected, members could be criticized and recalled if they proved to be incompetent. Chen Boda, Mao's personal secretary and ideological aide, argued in the Party's theoretical journal, the *Red Flag*, that 'the masses were the real masters of the Paris Commune'. In January 1967, groups of revolutionary activists, workers, peasants and students began seizing power from local Communist Party organizations and establishing communes on their own. The most famous of these was the Shanghai People's Commune, established in early February, although others were also established in Beijing, Taiyuan and Harbin. The *Red Flag* argued that, 'A completely new organizational form of political power better suited to the social economic base will be created.'[32]

The role of the Party in this new system, however, remained unclear. If Mao was to sanction the establishment of communes all across the country, then China would soon divide into independent kingdoms, destroying one foundation of the Party's *raison d'être*. Zhou Enlai pointed out that the communes had been established not through mass participation as was the case in the Paris Commune, but in the fervour of factional struggle. Mao therefore ordered Zhang Chunqiao, the ultra-leftist Shanghai leader, to change the name of his commune to the 'Shanghai Revolutionary Committee'. Zhang told 6,000 officials of Mao's decision: 'I believe we need it [the Communist Party] because we need a hard core, a bronze matrix, to strengthen us on the road we still have to travel. You can call it what you please, Communist Party or Socialist Party, but we must have a Party.'[33]

While Mao was effectively undermining the political strength of the Party, he briefly reallocated its role as the vanguard of the proletariat to the People's Liberation Army. While the army was Mao's most natural ally within the Party organization, he was fully aware that it should never be allowed to become an independent political power in its own right. 'Every communist must understand this truth,' Mao remarked at the Sixth Plenum of the Central Committee in 1938, 'political power grows out of the barrel of a gun. Our principle is that the Party commands the gun; the gun shall never be allowed to command the Party.'[34]

Mao's attack on the Party establishment began at the Ninth Congress of the Communist Youth League in June 1964, although a month earlier the General Political Department of the People's Liberation Army had published the first edition of *Quotations from Chairman Mao* – the 'Little Red Book' – which would become an omnipresent feature of the Cultural Revolution. The Youth League's role in the Cultural Revolution, and indeed the role of the Red Guards, was short but very effective. After the seizure of power in Shanghai and other major cities, Mao established provincial committees, based on a three-way alliance between the army, rectified Communist Party cadres and the revolutionary masses, who played a diminishing role.

Mao's aim in the Cultural Revolution went beyond the mere humbling of the existing bureaucratic and technocratic elite. He sought to extirpate the roots of any stratification which might emerge in the future, by destroying respect for the special status of Party members or for the special knowledge of a technocrat, thereby establishing the masses as the true source of all political authority.

By using the army against the bureaucracy, however, Mao had involved the military in the political process. In 1969, at the Ninth Party Congress, the army was allocated half of the seats on the Central Committee and Marshal Lin Biao was named as Mao's chosen successor. After Lin's disgrace, however, the army lost some of its prestige and concentrated once more on military matters. In 1969, having publicly humiliated Party cadres for being the enemies of their own revolution, Mao reaffirmed the Party as the decisive leadership organization: 'You are communists, you are that part of the masses which is more conscious, you are that part of the proletariat which is more conscious.'[35] While Mao was unwilling to instigate more Cultural Revolution-type campaigns before his death, he was still repelled by the thought of a bureaucratic society which had no active popular participation.

While centralism was thus important to Mao for guiding the revolution, democracy was essential if the revolution was to continue, and it was this voluntarism which is Mao's biggest theoretical contribution to Chinese society. Celebrating Stalin's sixtieth birthday in Yan'an in 1939, Mao had stated: 'There are innumerable principles of Marxism, but in the last analysis they can all be summed up in one sentence: "To rebel is justified".'[36] At the '7,000 Cadres Conference' in 1962, Mao had urged these Party workers, who were used to accepting the decisions of their higher authorities without questioning them, to accept the criticism of the people. 'Let others speak out. The heavens will not fall and you will not be thrown out. If you do not let others speak, then the day will surely come when you are thrown out.'[37] Mao's patent difficulty in getting this message across to the ordinary Chinese, even having to justify it by its foreign usage, brings home how heavy the dead-weight of traditional deference to authority is in China, even today.

Since Mao's death in 1976, the contradiction between centralism and democracy has continued. The Party's loss of face during the Cultural Revolution and the nasty experiences of today's leaders during the Cultural Revolution have resulted in contemporary policies which go against Mao's democratic voluntarism. Meanwhile the army, used by Mao as a weapon against the Party in the 1960s, has gained a more influential role since his death.

In 1976, Hua Guofeng was able to have the Gang of Four arrested, and thus dispose of one possible challenge to his authority, only because of the tacit support of the country's military commanders, especially Ye Jiangying. But when Hua went on to emphasize the need to 'grasp the key link of class struggle', the army, whose commanders had suffered as much as the technocrats from Mao's emphasis on class struggle, became the crucial factor in supporting Deng's challenge for the leadership. In 1982 the State Central Military Commission was created, and for the first time the People's Republic of China, rather than the Chinese Communist Party, had its own army.[38] In spite of this constitutional change, however, the army remains effectively an army of the Party, a situation inherited from the civil war era, and not, as the events of Tiananmen Square in 1989 proved, an army of the people.

In 1981, the Party Central Committee, in its *Resolution on Certain Questions in the History of Our Party Since the Founding of the People's Republic of China*, confessed that 'We failed to institutionalize and legalize inner-Party democracy and democracy in the political and social life of the country', and attributed this failing to the reasoning behind the Cultural Revolution.[39] Since 1979, under the revised Electoral Law, cases are routinely reported in the press of Communist Party-approved candidates who fail to win election in local people's congresses or unslated candidates nominated from the floor winning election to important posts. But, as Mao had feared, corrupt officials have enjoyed increased access to power, with potent factions being formed for corrupt purposes. Thus the Guangdong Provincial Communist Party Committee fell into the hands of the 'Swatow Gang', and the Guangzhou Municipal Communist Party Committee became controlled by the 'Maixian Gang'.

The People's Congresses became the centres of discussion of Party policy, but were used by both reformers and conservatives within the leadership to block each other's policies. At the

Thirteenth Congress, in 1987, Deng Liqun was nominated by
Chen Yun for a place on the Central Committee, but was voted
down by the Congress in a notable act of negative democracy.
While Deng Xiaoping wanted increased democratization of
society, his experience of mass participation outside the control
of the Communist Party during the Great Leap and the Cultural
Revolution have made him wary of implementing changes in the
Party's relation with society.

In a speech to the Hong Kong Basic Law Drafting Committee in 1987, Deng touched on his desire for increased
democratization:

> I told a foreign visitor that general elections may be held on
> the mainland in the next century, half a century hence. We
> now conduct indirect elections above the *xian* level. Direct
> elections are conducted only in the grassroots units at or
> below *xian* level. This is because we have a population of
> one billion, the people's cultural quality is also insufficient,
> and conditions are not ripe for practising direct elections.[40]

It is, of course, the Party that will decide when the conditions
are ripe for elections. It may be noted that Yang Zhongmei,
Hu Yaobang's biographer, judges Deng from his record since
the 1957 anti-rightist campaign, of which he was put in charge,
including the Democracy Wall movement of the late 1970s, to
be politically and ideologically 'inflexible and repressive'.[41]

After the Tiananmen Square massacre of 1989, Deng turned
away from the possibility of general elections, and stressed the
system of multi-party democracy that exists within China today.
In February 1990, he stated that the Chinese system

> is fundamentally different from the multi-party system or
> bipartisan system in the Western capitalist countries and also
> differs from the one-party system practised in some socialist
> countries. It was created by integrating Marxism-Leninism
> with China's revolution and construction, and is a socialist
> system of political parties that conform to China's conditions.
> To persist in and improve this system constitutes a major
> aspect of China's political restructuring.[42]

In highlighting the importance of the eight non-Communist political parties in China, each with a membership of roughly 50,000 (compared with the 48 million members of the Communist Party), Deng appears to be alluding to the united front policy of the Party immediately after 1949. 'The democratic parties,' he continues, 'should be turned from flower-vase parties into ones that take part in politics.' However, Deng's belief in the vanguard role of the Party remains unchanged. 'We will never allow democratic parties to become opposition parties. The ban on [opposition] parties should be maintained.'[43] While continuing to promote the idea of political reform, Deng's insistence on the importance of the Party, therefore, remains unaltered. In 1984 he remarked that 'the modernization process in a backward country needs strongman politics rather than Western-style democracy as a driving force'.[44]

Both Hu Yaobang and Zhao Ziyang, who owed their political power to Deng, attempted to implement democratic changes in China, and both suffered because of the power of the Party conservatives. Zhao's seven-point programme for political reform, presented to the Thirteenth Party Congress in 1987, contains many of the elements which Mao also saw as necessary to establish a socialist society. Zhao's programme promoted the separation of the Party and the state; the delegation of powers to lower levels; the reform of government organs; the reform of the personnel system, relating to the admittance of Party cadres; the establishment of a system of consultation and dialogue; the improvement of a number of systems relating to socialist democracy; and the strengthening of the legal system.

In the 1950s the state was vastly expanded in order to aid the construction of a socialist society. Its conservative effect on the Party, as we have seen, led Mao to emphasize the importance of continuous class struggle against those administrators showing bureaucratic tendencies. Statism is now seen by many of Zhao's supporters among the humanist Marxists, like Zhang Shuyi, as the 'root cause of all the defects of the old system'.[45] The first area in which the separation of the Party and the state has been achieved has been in the state's role in the economy. Here, Zhao argued, the state's role as a micro-economic manager and producer of goods and services should be curtailed, while its position as the macro-economic manager of the economy should be strengthened.

In the 1982 constitution, the People's Republic of China was described as a 'socialist state under the people's democratic dictatorship', rather than, as previously, a 'socialist state of the dictatorship of the proletariat'. This was intended to incorporate as many people as possible into society, and thereby limit the potential number of enemies of the state. As the Communist Party moved back from the limelight in the economic sphere, so the state moved into centre stage; the 1982 constitution reverted to the 1954 constitution where the power of the Communist Party was hidden in kid gloves.

Zhao's fall, however, strengthened the position of those in the Party who believe in the continued importance of the Party's role within society. Ultimately, the separation of Party and state challenged the idea of the dictatorship of the proletariat and, more importantly, the vanguard role of the Party. In October 1989, the *People's Daily* quoted Deng as saying that 'socialist democracy, as a unity of the new democracy and the new dictatorship, must steadfastly maintain the unity between democracy and dictatorship, centralization and legality'.[46]

In an editorial the following month, the *People's Daily* agreed with the new Party Secretary General, Jiang Zemin, when he underlined the centrality of economic factors in determining China's future. But the Party, it continued, had become divorced from the masses, and it was essential for cadres to adhere to the 'mass-line' and take the lead in practising austerity and plain living. It was also necessary to strengthen democratic centralism and the collective leadership of Party committees at all levels. For Jiang, the necessary key to this increased theoretical awareness lay in the study of Marxism-Leninism-Mao Zedong Thought, because it offered the means of resolving the fundamental contradiction between the implementation of the four cardinal principles and the practice of bourgeois liberalization.[47] Even Deng has continued to stress the importance of the political role of the Party. In 1986 he admitted that, 'In the final analysis, all our other reforms depend on the success of the political reform, because it is human beings who will – or will not – carry them out.'[48]

Deng therefore promotes the idea of a responsible and responsive Party, but not a Party which allows any dilution of its leading role. The problems for the Party within China now are considerable. Mao's Gutian Resolution of 1929, which described the role of the Party in strictly Leninist terms as a vanguard party, but mixed with Mao's characteristic mass radicalism, led to a number of contradictions. The economic reforms of the 1980s saw the re-emergence of the urban class structures of the 1950s, and many of the losers in the reform process were government administrators and workers. This has resulted in student and intellectual protests, worker strikes and the slowing down of productivity and increased cadre corruption.

The State Economic Restructuring Institute noted in 1988 that 'the masses' expectations of the benefits they can gain from the reform keep rising in a straight line', while 'the level of the masses' subjective appraisal of the improvement of their living standards keeps decreasing'. Chen Xiankui, writing in the *Guangming Daily*, took this argument to its logical conclusion in August 1988: 'The "complications" that have arisen with the times are profoundly transforming and shaking society as a whole. A slight carelessness in this regard will throw reform into the whirlpool of turbulence.'[49] In 1986 the urban population accounted for 37 per cent of China's total population, but the Communist Party, despite its role as the mouthpiece of the urban proletariat, has been unable successfully to represent this section of the population.

Within urban society, furthermore, there has been a growing contradiction between the working class and the Party. The 1983 constitution of the trade unions makes them independent within Party-defined boundaries, which could lead to a conflict of interests. In late 1983, a union spokesman commented that the 'division of labour and diversification of economic undertakings do create special interests'. In particular 'workers' special interests' could be encroached upon by the 'bureaucracy, unhealthy tendencies and unlawful practices'.

The emergence of special interest groups was recognized by the reformers. Zhao Ziyang, speaking at the Thirteenth Congress, declared that: 'Socialist society is not a monolith. In this society, people of all kinds, of course, share common interests, but their special interests should not be overlooked. The conflicting interests should be reconciled. The government should work to co-ordinate various kinds of interests and contradictions; the Party committee must be even better at the co-ordinating work.'[50] The Communist Party, in these cases, should therefore act with 'partisan neutrality', even though its political legitimacy rests on its position as the mouthpiece of the proletariat.

Zhao's attempts to reform the power of the bureaucracy, as the insistence on 'partisan neutrality' suggests, have been hindered by those elements within the Party which refuse to allow a weakening in its vanguard role. In Shaanxi province the problem focused on the traditional sources of power, the control of personnel appointments and the distribution of goods and services. Local leaders naturally stress the supremacy of the Party in the separation process, but display an inherent inability to let slip the reins of power. Wang Maolin, the deputy Party Secretary of Shaanxi Provincial Communist Party, argued that: 'It is not the purpose of local Party committees to rigidly share power with local governments, people's congresses, or the Chinese People's Political Consultative Committee . . . It is not appropriate to establish several highest decision-making centres. Pluralistic power structures at the same level will not work.'[51]

Thus, instead of a 'concentric circle metaphor', what we saw in existence in the 1980s was what Yang Zhongmei calls 'an autocratic pyramid, in which power is held by a small group of men at the top of the pyramid'.[52] Mao Zedong's blend of autocratic leadership with the 'mass-line' led to his giving more attention to popular opinion than many of his colleagues. This never went against the principle of the Party as the vanguard of the revolution, because it was not a question of submitting problems to arbitration by the masses, but of allowing them at most to 'make suggestions' (*ti-yijian* – implying a carefully restrained element of criticism) in accordance with Mao's 'mass-line' doctrine.

Mass participation in the Great Leap faltered because planning and co-ordination were a virtual impossibility given the political strength of the centre. Mass participation in the

Cultural Revolution succeeded in destroying those in the Party who were against democracy, but failed to resolve the underlying contradiction inherent in the organizational structure of Chinese society. When Mao's theoretical arguments had reached their logical conclusion, as they did in the establishment of the Shanghai Commune in 1967, he was forced to reinstate the position of the Party and thereby negate the influence of mass democracy.

The success of Mao's emphasis on the 'mass-line' was that it helped to break down the servile attitude of the Chinese people towards authority. Since the Cultural Revolution, all the mass movements in Chinese society, from the Tiananmen Square demonstrations of 1976, through the Democracy Wall protests in 1979 and the de-collectivization of the peasant economy, to the major Tiananmen Square demonstrations of 1989, have been the result of mass spontaneity, outside the dictates of Party policy. This voluntarism has yet to find a suitable outlet within Chinese Communist ideology, however, and the Party has always reverted to increased centralism, and the promotion of the Party line, after each outburst of mass protest.

Mao tried to use the masses to improve the democratic nature of the Chinese Communists, while Zhao looked more at the Party's relationship with the state, attacking the democracy–centralism contradiction from above. Liao Gailong, a member of the Party Secretariat and a close aide to Deng Xiaoping, pointed out in 1980 that Lenin's ideas about organization and the role of the Party (encapsulated in his *What is to be Done*) reflected the pre-revolutionary oppression of Tsarist Russia, leading Lenin to emphasize centralism at the expense of democracy, and assert the proletarian dictatorship as an 'iron' dictatorship not bound by any laws. 'This dictatorship,' Liao commented, 'over-emphasized the role of force and emphasized not being bound by anything. Thus the power of the Party and the state became over-centralized in the hands of the Central Committee of the Communist Party and finally became over-centralized in the hands of one or two leaders.'[53]

Although the current return to the concept of a primary stage of socialism echoes Mao's *On New Democracy*, the events of the past forty years have been too profound for a simple turning back of the clock to start again. The historical significance of the 1980s is that a synthesis was slowly emerging. Having attempted to promote democracy from below, through Mao's mass radicalism, and democracy from above, through the reforms of Zhao Ziyang and Hu Yaobang, the Communist Party finds itself caught in the trap of the contradiction between democracy and centralism. The most important axiom of this primary stage of socialism continues to be the role of the Chinese Communist Party as the 'ruling party' in society. The contradictions that this entails, however, ensure that the Party will continue to be unable to unite democracy and centralism into a stable and effective system of government.

3 *State vs. Market* –
The Question of the Economy

Four out of every five Chinese are peasants, and farming has been the mainstay of the Chinese economy for over two thousand years. During the reign of Emperor Han Wuti, one of the first promoters of the Confucian system of government, imperial decrees began with the words – 'The world is based on agriculture'.[1] The peasants played an indispensable role in the communists' victory in the civil war, but their role in the new society that followed could be fulfilled politically only if they played their part economically, and that required the socialization of agriculture, co-ordinated with the development of a powerful industry with state enterprise as its backbone. This process, however, necessitated a change in the feudalistic thinking upon which the Han empire had been founded.

The importance which Mao Zedong attached to economic policy can be seen from the fact that fifteen out of the thirty ministerial posts created by the People's Consultative Conference in 1949 were concerned with economic affairs. Soon after the establishment of the People's Republic, Mao observed: 'The serious task of economic construction is ahead of us. Things in which we were well versed will soon be needed no longer, and we shall have to do things in which we are not versed. This is our trouble.'[2] Inflation, which had raged during the civil and Japanese wars, reached a nightmare 1,100 per cent towards the end of 1948, and in Shanghai in the first few months of 1949 it escalated to the incredible rate of 163,700 per cent. Public confidence was quite destroyed, and the foreign-exchange rate for the gold *yuan*, which had stood at four per US dollar in mid-1948, rocketed to 205,000 per US dollar by April 1949.[3]

The civil war, following so closely on the heels of the Sino–Japanese War and a series of natural disasters, had brought about a grave food shortage. If the new government was to gain any credibility with the people, it had to be seen to be taking positive steps to control the economy and promote redevelopment and growth. 'The two basic policies of the state in the economic struggle,' Mao announced to the Second Plenum of the Seventh Central Committee in 1949, 'will be the regulation of capital at home and control of foreign trade.'[4]

Urban areas were not to be solely political centres of power, they also had to be the economic foundation and base for the new China. The Second Plenum stated, in March 1949, that 'the key point in administering and building up the cities is the rehabilitation and development of industrial production: first, the production of public-owned enterprises; second, that of private enterprises; and, third, handicraft production'.[5] In the new democratic state, private capitalism would be allowed to exist, so that modernization could occur. 'Big banks, big industries and big business shall be owned by this Republic . . . At the same time, however, the state will not confiscate other capitalist private property and will not forbid the development of capitalist production that "cannot manipulate the people's livelihood". This is because the Chinese economy is still in a very backward state.'[6]

Just as the national bourgeoisie and the petty bourgeoisie fell within the political boundaries of the Party's united front policy, so they were included in the Party's economic system, as long as they were oriented constructively towards the domestic economy. The aim was to ensure that the business community would become more united with the state and more inward-looking, developing industrial and agricultural modernization for China's benefit. The state's initial role was to be that of guide, pointing the businessmen in the right direction towards a socialist economy developed from inside with minimal foreign involvement.

In the urban areas the Party implemented a series of anti-inflationary policies, which gradually brought the economy back under control. A new currency was issued, duplicity of function within the state bureaucracy was avoided and austerity promoted, while the people were made to pay more taxes and encouraged to save with the new state-owned banks. The Party began rebuilding the infrastructure which had been so damaged by the years of war to allow local markets throughout the country to be transformed into a national single market, enabling state planning to be more effective. By the beginning of 1950, some 20,490 kilometres or 78 per cent of the railway capacity had been restored, while the People's Liberation Army were mobilized under the slogan 'Extend the highway lines where the People's Army goes'[7].

In the industrial sector, the government gave loans to factories in both the public and private sectors, but funds were limited. The Party looked to improve productivity through industrial efficiency, for example by controlling labour–capital disputes and organizing labour. One problem the Party faced when it arrived in the towns and cities was that workers had taken Communist propaganda too literally, and a series of strikes threatened the whole policy of economic construction. In August 1949, the Shanghai Military Control Commission issued an order permitting businesses to close, allowing employers to sack incompetent or unsatisfactory workers and setting reasonable limits on severance pay.

Disputes between labour and capital which could not be solved within the factory went to arbitration by the Municipal Labour Bureau, or, on appeal, to the People's Court, and workers were forbidden to enter factories to 'obstruct management by mob tactics'. This, however, did not mean that the workers were to be kept in an inferior position. As the New China News Agency reported in May 1950, 'in publicly-owned enterprises, the working class is in a position of leadership; in private enterprises the position of the working class is that of equality with the capitalist.'[8]

New trade-union and other worker organizations were involved in the promotion of efficiency. In November 1949 the government announced the first in a series of mass mobilization campaigns, to give 'handsome rewards to workers who discover ways and means to cut down on waste'.[9] The new draft Trade Union Law, announced in May 1950, included the statement that 'any organization or individual may submit opinions on the draft to the Ministry of Labour . . . and these will be taken into account before the draft becomes law'. This force of mass mobilization would be best utilized with good organization. Speaking about the mass movement, Li Fuzhun, Vice Chairman of the North East People's Government and one of the high economic mandarins of the early decades of Communist rule, stated that 'as a democratic movement of the broad masses it must also develop the businesslike running of enterprises with democratization of administration'.[10]

While the Party emphasized the importance of currency stability and industrial production, the basis of the economy still lay in the agricultural sector. In traditional Chinese folklore, a government was acceptable if the *lao bai xing*, or the bulk of the peasantry, had enough food to eat. In October 1947, the Basic Agrarian Law had sanctioned the full-scale mobilization of the Party and army behind a programme of land confiscation and redistribution, including the confiscation of all land of rich peasants and landlords.[11] By 1949 this view had been modified, and the first stage in the agri-socialization process was envisaged as incorporating free competition among peasants. The consequent appearance of new rich peasants and capitalist farmers was to be emphasized as a means of raising production. The state would keep these capitalist tendencies under control through government directives and the use of peasant associations at the local level.

The lesson which the Communists had learnt during the Yan'an period, from 1937 to 1945, and the ensuing civil war, was to delay land reform until conditions were right. In the older 'liberated' areas, land redistribution had started as early as 1947, but in the newly liberated areas rent reduction was first imposed and land redistribution not scheduled until the autumn of 1950. Just as Mao emphasized the importance of correct leadership in politics, in the form of the doctrine of the mass-line, so he also wanted to ensure that traditional agrarian cultural norms would be broken down before the Party attempted to implement land reform. This meant that the masses would have to show that they wanted the land to be redistributed, and, more importantly, that Party control over the process was secure.[12]

In the foreign economic arena, the problem still remained for the Communists of finding a suitable injection of capital investment for the modernization of industry. Rather than utilizing foreign capital, expertise and technology, the Chinese Communists felt that the essential precondition for effective development was in breaking the grip of foreign domination over the economy. In his speech, *On the People's Democratic Dictatorship*, in 1949, Mao gave an indication of the importance of self-reliance which he would later apply rigidly to the Chinese economy. 'The imperialists reckon that we will not be able to manage our economy; they are standing by and looking on, awaiting our failure.'[13]

This suspicion of Western motives was a major problem. Mao explained in this same speech that American or British aid would only be available 'because the capitalists of these countries want to make money and the bankers want to earn interest to relieve their own crisis; that would be no aid to the Chinese people'.[14] The initial emphasis was not, therefore, on autarky, but on control of foreign trade. This was achieved through laws ordering Chinese corporations to divest themselves of foreign capital by June 1950, and by the control of the customs, not only as a source of government revenue, but also to ensure that foreign commodities already produced in China would have high tariff duties unless they were essential to production.

Export-led industrialization was shunned as a design by the Western capitalist countries to perpetuate the thraldom of the Third World. China's need for technological aid had to be met from another source, the Soviet Union, and this ensured that the First Five Year Plan, which was finally launched at the beginning of 1954, was heavily influenced by Soviet industrialization ideas.

Some of the key features of the Chinese Communists' economic theory can nevertheless be discerned in these initial policies. Development was not to be measured in terms of higher gross national product or per capita income, but in a fuller realization of human and natural potential. Technology was important, but the most critical factor in the economy was human consciousness. The Party's role was to instil in the Chinese people, of whom the majority worked in agriculture, the belief that by working together and adapting technology for the community's need, they could improve their livelihood. As one worker put it after 1949: 'In the old days the machines came first, and we were their servants. Now we are the masters, we make them work for us.'[15]

The First Five Year Plan announced the necessary conditions for the 'planned economic construction and gradual transition to socialism'. The envisaged pace of transformation remained modest, and in his opening address to the First Session of the National People's Congress in 1954, Mao stated that it would require 'several five-year plans' to turn China into a highly industrialized country. Four years later, however, this mood of moderation gave way to the cultivation of haste. In his speech to the Supreme State Conference in January 1958, Mao predicted that 'we shall catch up with Britain in fifteen years; we shall produce forty million tons of steel annually . . .'[16]

The reasoning behind the change in pace derived from agriculture. In 1950, Liu Shaoqi had stated that the 'rich peasant economy' would be preserved 'throughout the whole stage of New Democracy', to be superseded 'only when the conditions are mature for the extensive application of mechanized farming, for the organization of collective farms and for the socialist reform of the rural areas'. All this, he added, 'will take a somewhat long time to achieve'.[17]

During the First Five Year Plan, agriculture had taken a back seat to industry, which had been emphasized even more than in the first Soviet Five Year Plan (1929–34), because, according to the Chinese Communists, virtually all of China's industry lay in or around the coastal cities, vulnerable to foreign attack. Gradually, however, the rural mutual aid teams of the First Five Year Plan were developed into semi-socialist agrarian producer co-operatives. In a speech in July 1955, Mao called for a sharp increase in the rate of agricultural collectivization, which he rationalized as the best method of providing the infrastructure for increased agricultural productivity – upon which the industrialization process depended.

In endeavouring to apply Marxist economic principles to the Chinese economy, Mao was again faced with the problem of reconciling the backward nature of Chinese society with Marxist historiography. In 1938, this had led Mao to call for the Sinification of Marxism, and in 1955 he began to apply this to the Chinese economy. Just as he had looked to the peasantry to provide the essential support for the success of the revolution, so now he turned to agriculture to provide the engine of China's economic growth.

In 1956 Mao produced his most important speech on the economy, entitled *On the Ten Major Relationships*. Of the ten 'problems' which Mao addressed, five were directly concerned with the economy – the relationship between industry and agriculture, and between heavy and light industry; the relationship between industry in the coastal regions and industry in the interior; the relationship between economic construction and defence construction; the relationship between the state, the units of production and the individual producers; and the relationship between the Centre and the regions. 'These relationships,' Mao emphasized, 'are contradictions', and therefore they would, according to Mao's philosophical interpretation of Marxism, provide the necessary motor of change in China's economic development.

At the Eighth Party Congress in 1956, Mao rejected the idea of market socialism and declared that the principal contradiction in society was between the 'advanced socialist system' and the 'backward productive forces'.[18] The solution, therefore, lay in injecting economic theory with Mao's theory of uninterrupted revolution. Thus, Mao's emphasis on the primacy of class struggle in the political arena was transferred into the economic arena, so that the dynamic force behind economic modernization becomes the resolution of these contradictions in society through the method of permanent revolution.

The Great Leap Forward, which was officially launched in 1958, was the first step in this process of envisaging economic modernization in comprehensive economic, political and social terms. During 1956–7, the Chinese Communists had drafted their Second Five Year Plan, loosely following the gradualist approach of the First Plan. The two Plans were essentially economic, but the Great Leap, which superseded the Second Plan, was based on Mao's dialectical conception of Chinese society and encompassed all factors of societal dynamics. The Great Leap slogan was *zhengzhi guashuai* – 'politics takes command'.[19] Whereas the First Five Year Plan had been analysed in standard technical terms, the development model of the Great Leap included ideological analyses, seeing the economy in dialectical, as well as technical, terms. Thus, every element in the economy had a corresponding contradictory element.

The most illuminating catchphrase to emerge from the Great Leap was 'simultaneous development'. In the first of Mao's ten great relationships, the contradiction between industry and agriculture, and between light and heavy industry, can be recognized the idea of sectoral contradiction, which has been a persistent train of thought in Chinese Communist ideology. The basis of this dialectical approach was that the promotion of heavy industry as the primary sector in economic modernization would result in unbalanced and therefore inferior development. Mao now rebutted this in his speech *On the Ten Great Relationships*: 'Developing heavy industry on a foundation of satisfying the needs of the people's livelihood, will provide a more solid foundation for the development of heavy industry, and the result will be to develop it more and better.'[20]

For the Chinese Communists, the differentiation between heavy and light industry was not in terms of producer versus consumer goods, but in political terms. What the Chinese saw as heavy industry were those industries which were strategically important for development goals and therefore a priority for state investment. Whatever remained was referred to as light industry. By the Great Leap Forward, the government was faced with a 'scissors' crisis, with unfavourable terms of trade between agriculture and heavy and light industry. Peasants hoarded their goods, and farm output fell off. Light industry had been starved of the reinvestment capital necessary for modernization, the farmers had nothing to buy and no incentive to produce, and so the whole accumulation programme of the government was threatened.

The triangular relationship between these three sectors of the economy, heavy industry, light industry and agriculture, was therefore broken down into a series of dialectics. In 1963 the *Jingji Yanjin* explained this dialectical process.

A [priority] sequence of agriculture, light industry, heavy industry means that the unified state economic plan must proceed from the agriculture plan. Starting out from the development of agriculture, one can proceed toward the development of our country's socialist construction. Moreover, on the basis of the capacities and needs of agriculture, one can arrange the development plans of light and heavy industry (including scale, speed and composition) and achieve comprehensive balance, thereby assuring maximally rapid proportionate development of the national economy.[21]

During the 1950s, the importance of each of these sectors in this triangular relationship followed the priority of heavy industry, light industry and agriculture. After the disaster of the Great Leap, during which each sector was supposed to have equal weight attached to it, the 1960s saw the emphasis change to light industry, agriculture and heavy industry. In the 1970s light industry remained the top priority, followed by heavy industry and then agriculture. After 1978, agricultural growth was helped by the success of light industry, but by the mid-1980s investment in heavy industry had once more increased and its growth rate surpassed that of agriculture. This dichotomy between industry and agriculture, as well as the intra-industrial dualism between light and heavy industry, has been a persistent feature of the Chinese economy since 1949.

Another sectoral contradiction which Mao identified in his speech in 1957 was that between the coastal areas and the interior. This relates to the difference between modern industry, represented by the technological heavy industrial areas in Shanghai and north-east China, and traditional industry based on longstanding production methods in the inland areas. The concern about the gap between the coast and the interior was partly ideological, and partly because the Communist leaders were all inland-born. The interior had been one of the backbones of the revolutionary cause, and although it had gone through a social revolution, with land reform and the collectivization of agriculture, the economic benefits of Communist policy had not been tangible. The dualistic approach of the Great Leap, especially its concept of the back-yard steel furnace in every community, was the proposed solution to these problems.

The most important contradiction in the Great Leap, however, was between the dynamics of change. The gradualist approach, favoured by Liu Shaoqi, promoted the orthodox Marxist view that the mechanization of agriculture should be accomplished before collectivization. During the collectivization campaign of 1955–6, Mao stressed the importance of changes in mentality and atmosphere, so that the 'conscious action' of humans, released through class struggle, could be the motor behind economic development.

In his notes to a book entitled *Socialist Upsurge in China's Countryside*, in 1955, Mao noted that

> Political work is the lifeline of economic work. This is particularly true at a time when the economic and social system is undergoing a fundamental change. The agricultural co-operative movement, from the very beginning, has been a severe ideological and political struggle. No co-operative can be established without going through such a struggle. Before a brand-new social system can be built on the site of the old, the site must first be swept clean. Old ideas reflecting the old system unavoidably remain in people's heads for a long time. They do not easily give way.

'The basic requirement of political work,' Mao added in another note, 'is constantly to imbue the peasant masses with a socialist ideology and to criticize capitalist tendencies.'[22]

Lenin had also had faith in voluntarism, but his belief in the power of the human will to transform reality was manifested primarily in the domain of politics. Stalin's collectivization drive in the USSR in 1929 was backed by the theory that although there were only few tractors in the rural areas, the basis of agricultural industry had already been laid, and thus the productive forces were already in place. Mao argued that this process should develop the other way round. 'The country's economic conditions being what they are, the technical transformation will take somewhat longer than the social.'[23] The emphasis, therefore, should be on human transformation.

During the First Five Year Plan, the Chinese Communists had relied upon capital rather than labour-intensive modes of operation, even though the factor endowment of the Chinese economy in 1949 had been its abundance of agricultural labour. The Great Leap saw the implementation of the idea of the maximum utilization of labour, with China's vast population being viewed as an asset and not a liability. The use of human resources was an example of the resolution of this contradiction. The aim of the communes, economically, was to speed up development of the country by providing the administrative framework for the organization of human labour to replace scarce machines, and cultivate the land in units large enough to facilitate the introduction of machinery.

For Mao, voluntarism was not exclusively applicable to politics, as it had been for Lenin and Stalin. The Great Leap saw this theory being extended to the realm of nature. 'Many living examples show that there is only unproductive thought, there are no unproductive regions. There are only poor methods for cultivating the land, there is no such thing as poor land. Provided only that people manifest in full measure their subjective capacities for action, it is possible to modify natural conditions.'[24]

Mao knew full well how backward the Chinese economy was. In January 1958, he stated that: 'Whenever we talk about it, we say that our country has such an enormous population, it has such a vast territory, abundant resources, so many people, four thousand years of history and culture . . . We have bragged so much about this, yet we cannot compare with a country like Belgium.' His solution to China's backwardness lay in releasing the energy of the people – 'Ours is an ardent nation now swept by a burning tide. There is a good metaphor for this; our nation is like an atom . . . When this atom's nucleus is smashed, the thermal energy which is released will have really tremendous power. We shall be able to do things which we could not do before.'[25]

Mao's mentality and approach to economic affairs were fully revealed in the Great Leap Forward. After an inspection trip around the countryside at the end of 1958, he stated that he had 'witnessed the tremendous energy of the masses. On this foundation it is possible to accomplish any task whatsoever.'[26] He was denounced by some of his colleagues for the steel production techniques of the Great Leap Forward, which they referred to as a guerrilla habit. To orthodox Marxists, and to the Russians in particular, Mao appeared to be turning Marxism-Leninism on its head. Alan Winnington, the British reporter who had settled in China after the Korean War, criticized the idealism behind Mao's theories, by quoting from Marx: 'It is not consciousness that decides our existence but social being that determines our consciousness.'[27]

The official communiqué of the Lushan Plenum, which was held in 1959 as a post-mortem on the Great Leap, recognized that the figures published for economic achievement during the first year of the Great Leap had been exaggerated by between 40 per cent and 50 per cent. The bad harvest of 1959, following so closely after the fragmentation and disorganization of the peasant economy, resulted in three years of the worst famine since the Communists came to power. The crisis was surmounted by keeping the communes as administrative units, while economic control was handed back to the 'production team' – effectively the old 'mutual aid team' which had conducted agriculture in the early 1950s. The accent on industry in economic planning was corrected and it was formally recognized that agriculture formed the basis of the national economy.

The commune consisted of approximately a hundred villages, or about 50,000 people; it was the highest unit of agriculture and lowest unit of government all in one. There were three tiers in it: the Production Team, based on the old village; the Production Brigade, equivalent to the Co-operative of the mid-1950s; and the commune itself, which could be utilized for projects, for example, irrigation works, which required such a mass of labour.

To many Western commentators, the communes appeared to demonstrate the irrationality of Chinese Communism. Pots and pans were collectivized, communal mess halls were constructed, and even separate dormitories were set up for men and women. These, however, were the extreme cases. In fact such early experiments represented a tiny fraction of the communes, and were discouraged by Beijing after a few weeks when their inapplicability became apparent. In reality, it was the worries, for example, of an old peasant in Zhou Libo's celebrated novel of 1958, *Great Changes in a Mountain Village*, which thwarted the radicalization of the commune policy. 'No matter how you look at it,' he confides to his wife, 'I cannot bear to give up the few pieces of hill land.'[28] Similarly, the challenge of the back-yard steel furnaces, which were intended seriously to augment national production, was left to amateurs and the products largely wasted.

While Mao now left the running of economic affairs to his more pragmatic colleagues in the Central Committee, he still held by the views that had resulted in the chaos after the Great Leap. In 1966 he wrote that, while in general the material determines the mental, ideas can influence the economic base. This policy failed in the Great Leap Forward because it set out to change the material mode of production without changing the superstructure of ideas. The solution lay with the Cultural Revolution which would ensure that capitalist and feudalist ideas were replaced by Mao's correct interpretation of Marxism-Leninism.

In 1967, in an editorial in the *People's Daily*, Mao observed that:

> Some muddle-headed people counterpose the revolution to production and think that once the Great Cultural Revolution starts, it will impede production. Therefore, they take hold of production alone and do not grasp the revolution. These comrades have not thought through the question of what is the purpose of farming, of weaving, of steelmaking. Is it for building socialism, or is it for building capitalism?[29]

Mao wanted to check consumerism, so that investment would be released for the long-term and a capitalist consumer society would be established. The economy was indeed impeded and slowed down as a result of the Cultural Revolution, but there was no repetition of the food scarcity which had blackened the Great Leap.

Mao's vision of economic development as a spiral process in which political mobilization and cultural change are the conditions and concomitants of industrialization collided with rational methods of development. 'The overall result,' according to Stuart Schram, 'is a zigzag evolution in which the emphasis is periodically shifted from the difficulties hindering the industrialization of a backward country to the extraordinary force inherent in all newly liberated peoples, and especially in the Chinese people, which makes them capable of triumphing over all obstacles.'[30]

In the 1960s, however, with China isolated from both the capitalist and socialist countries, the Communists, and Mao in particular, looked to the Chinese people themselves to provide the momentum behind national development. In 1962, Mao reminisced about the situation the Communist leadership had faced immediately after the establishment of the People's Republic in 1949. 'In economic construction we were as children, lacking experience; unfamiliar with tactics and strategy, we made war on the earth.'[31] The short-term solution lay in copying the development pattern of the Soviet Union. 'At that time it was absolutely necessary to act thus, but at the same time it was also a weakness – a lack of creativity and a lack of the ability to stand on our own feet. Naturally this could not be our long-term strategy.'[32]

The Sino–Soviet split in 1960, when the USSR suddenly withdrew all its technical advisers and capital from China, forced Mao into a drastic reassessment of Marxist economic theory. For Marx, the only salvation for the backward and stagnant societies of Asia was a full-scale 'Europeanization' process, based on the strength of the working class in Europe, and on Marx's conviction that only European culture possessed the necessary Promethean thrust that would enable non-European countries to achieve economic development through their own working class. For Mao, this implied that Chinese people were inferior to the West, especially to the Soviet Union. In 1970, he told Edgar Snow that the Russians 'looked down on the Chinese and also looked down on the peoples of many other countries'.[33]

The impetus for change, then, would come not from urban areas, as Marx had suggested, but from the Chinese peasantry, who represented the majority of the population. By the beginning of the 1970s, however, China had reached an economic plateau from which Mao's policies of 'hard struggle and self-reliance' would lead only to diminished returns. Gross national product per capita increased by between 2 per cent and 2.5 per cent per annum between 1957 and 1977, in spite of the 2 per cent annual population increase (which was higher than the average of 1.5 per cent for the rest of the Third World). Net output of industry increased by 10.2 per cent per annum between 1957 and 1979, almost double the average of 5.4 per cent in other low-income countries. The World Bank regarded 'China's most remarkable achievement over these decades as making its low-income groups far better off in terms of basic needs compared with their counterparts in most other poor countries'.[34]

Average Chinese incomes were increasing more slowly than GNP in the urban areas, however, and hardly at all in the countryside, with the lion's share of national income being used for investment rather than being passed back to producers to stimulate consumption. Peasants had thus been starved of investment funds, and the desired modernization process in the countryside had faltered because of the lack of technology. In the 1950s, the Chinese were able to use Soviet technology, before turning to West European countries and Japan for technological imports in the early 1960s. In terms of high technology, the Chinese achieved much, for example in the development of their own nuclear bomb, but in the rural areas the reliance on human consciousness had reached its zenith.

Between 1971 and 1973, the Chinese government turned to the United States for machinery and equipment. This, in turn, led to the open-door policies of the present leadership, which some commentators present as evidence of the failure of China's policy of self-reliance. Mao was fiercely nationalistic, but not xenophobic. Foreign things, he stressed, should be adapted to fit Chinese conditions and serve Chinese needs, and this could be done only if the Chinese shed the inferiority complex which the years of imperialist encroachment in China had instilled in them.

In the 1960s Mao had been obliged to re-examine traditional Chinese culture in order to find an economic solution to China's development problems. In 1965, in Hangzhou, he reversed his earlier opinion that 'Marxism is a fundamental theory which was produced in the West. How then can we make a distinction between what is Chinese and what is Western in this respect?'[35] Instead he said: 'We cannot adopt Western learning as the substance, nor can we use the substance of the democratic republic. We cannot use the "rights of man" nor the "theory of evolution". We can only use Western technology.'[36]

In the 1980s, China's leaders stressed that their open-door policy was not a sign of 'worshipping things foreign and fawning upon foreigners', 'begging from imperial countries' or 'turning China into the imperialists' dumping ground', as the radicals in the Communist Party complained. Rather, the importing of foreign technology is now hailed as the confirmation of Mao's teaching about 'making things foreign serve China'.[37] Yuan Mu, the State Council spokesman, stated in September 1990 that, 'As Chairman Mao said, we should rely mainly on our own efforts while seeking external assistance as auxiliary.'[38] What has changed since Mao was in power is that Western technology, and, more importantly, Western finance, has been made readily available to the Chinese leaders.

The importance of Western technology, and the establishment of many Hong Kong, Japanese and Western joint venture companies within the Special Economic Zones in China, has once again raised the question of the contradiction between China's coastal cities and the interior. During the Cultural Revolution, when an imminent Soviet or American attack on China was a constant theme of the leadership, preparations for war led to the adoption of a strategy of regional industrial autarky. The share of the industrial production of the coastal provinces relative to the interior fell from 69 per cent in 1952 to 61 per cent in 1978. The 'third-line construction' policies of the Cultural Revolution, however, are unlikely to be repeated.

The open-door policy has increased the gap between the coast and the interior, as foreigners have preferred the coastal regions because of the existence of infrastructure and corporate economies, and this has led to increased technological bifurcation. Zhao's answer to the contradiction between the coastal areas and the interior is that the open-door theory should be 'progressively extended from the special economic zones and coastal cities . . . to coastal economic regions, and finally to the interior areas'.[39] The purpose of the SEZs, according to the economist Ji Chongwei, should be to act as 'filters between China's social system and the capitalist world, allowing market mechanisms and the law of value to operate under the guidance of a socialist planned economy and taking in positive things and sifting out the negative aspects of Western culture'.[40]

The state's role in this process is paramount. In his *On the Ten Great Relationships*, Mao identified the triangular relationship between the state, the co-operative and the individual as one of the principal contradictions within Chinese society. The failure of the Great Leap Forward led to a partial dismantling of the peasant communes, with individual initiative being given more leeway by the government. Mao's economic policies failed because his repeated demands for the decentralization of economic decision-making and a shift from industry to agriculture were largely cancelled out by the imposition of inflexible policies from above and the discouragement of the traditional peasant market economy.

The historic decision of the Third Plenum of the Eleventh Central Committee in 1978 to raise the state grain purchase price by 20 per cent, with an additional 50 per cent for any grain produced over the allocated quota, became the starting point of a debate over the contradiction between the market and the state plan which persisted throughout the 1980s. It has become epitomized in the differences between Deng Xiaoping and Chen Yun, one of the few economic theorists within the Party leadership, whose views began to diverge in the mid-1980s as the programme of reforms rolled on. The cautious Chen, who had disagreed with the policies of the Great Leap, and thus fallen from favour with Mao, has consistently preferred a gradualist approach. 'We must be prudent and practical,' he warned in 1958, 'go forward slowly, gather experiences, push ahead gradually.'[41]

In 1979, Chen Yun, who opposes the elevation of the market into a position of equality with the state plan, seeing the market's role as merely a place for the exchange of local and less essential products, produced his famous 'bird cage' theory.

While reviving the economy, we must guard against the tendency to diverge from the state plan. Revitalization should be under the guidance of the plan; it should not depart from the plan. This can be compared with the relationship between a bird and its cage. A bird cannot be held tightly in one's hand because that would kill it; it must be allowed to fly. But it can only fly within the cage; without the cage it will escape. If the bird represents economic revitalization, then the cage represents state planning.[42]

Deng's theories have been summarized in his 'Four Cardinal Principles', which were upheld in 1980 as Zhou Enlai's bequest to the nation, after he proposed them in 1964 with Mao's backing. Deng's reform proposals in 1978–9, however, bore a strong resemblance to Lenin's New Economic Policy at the start of the Soviet Union, which saved the USSR from economic collapse by allowing the growth of a considerable sector of private enterprise. The 1981 *Resolution on Certain Questions of Party History* defined the Communists' post-Mao economic strategy: 'We must carry out the planned economy on the basis of a system of public ownership, while at the same time developing the subsidiary role of market adjustments.'[43]

Reformers within the Communist Party argued that the capitalism practised in Japan and the West in the 1980s, with some economic planning, anti-monopoly laws and social welfare legislation, is not as Marx and Lenin envisaged and this positive re-evaluation has enabled the Chinese Communists to borrow the techniques of capitalism to manage their commodity economy along the road to socialism. By the late 1980s economic theory had progressed from regarding the plan as primary and the market as secondary, to the unification of the two concepts, with the goal of a 'planned commodity economy' in which the 'law of value' would operate throughout the whole system, with an 'organic unity of planning and the market'. This enabled the Communists to view the means of production – industrial products, technology, finance, land and labour itself – as commodities in themselves.

The most important step along this road came in the agrarian sector. In 1985, *Document No. 1*, released by the Central Committee of the Party, said that the state would largely abandon its monopolistic procurement of agrarian produce.[44] Free markets would be encouraged to flourish, while the state retained a residual role, with the people being encouraged to 'swim in the billowing ocean of the commodity economy'. While the Third Plenum in 1978 had initiated the readjustment in the rural sector, *Document No. 1* is at the core of China's rural reforms. It may appear to repudiate Mao's idea of communization, yet it springs from the voluntarist policies on which he had based his vision of economic modernization.

One of the earliest decisions of the Third Plenum was to endorse a revised edition of the 1961 *Regulations on the Work in Rural People's Communes*, which epitomized a pragmatic approach to agricultural policy. The political differences between the two eras, however, can be seen in the main features of the 1978 decision – the decentralization of farm work, encouragement of private initiative and an emphasis on production for the market. Although the continuing validity of agriculture's collective framework was upheld, in reality contractual arrangements with groups and individuals became the focus of agricultural organization.

The first explicit, formal recognition of contractual arrangements with households as part of official policy was given in *Document No. 75*, which was released by the Central Committee in September 1980. By the end of that year, 30 per cent of all production teams had implemented household contracts of one form or another. Initially, the Party proposed two forms, *baochan daohu* (contracting output to the household) and *baogan daohu* (contracting everything to the household). The latter was the most radical, and was described as 'tenant farming with the collective and state as landlord'. By 1983, some 97 per cent of peasant households had embraced some form of contract system, with the *baogan daohu* being the most popular. The *People's Daily* warned against the abandonment of the public-ownership basis of the collective economy. 'Unchecked production in accordance with the dictates of short-run conditions of market demand,' it argued in 1982, 'is most likely to lead to an imbalance between supply and demand and the stockpiling of products, thereby causing losses to both state and peasants.'[45]

The emphasis on grain production was also dropped, and

by the mid-1980s 10 per cent of all peasant households were classified as 'specialized households', who were guaranteed grain supply and a specialized market for their goods. As long as technical progress and specialization conformed to certain conditions (land conservation, rational distribution, proper use and public accumulation of funds) then the old criticism that the household system was inherently inefficient and anti-modernization could be refuted. Indeed, the *Document No. 1* of 1985 should be seen as a reaction by the Party to the enthusiasm of the peasantry for reform – in other words, the peasantry had provided the necessary impetus for change, as Mao had predicted, but not in the way he had expected.

The Eighth Five Year Plan, covering 1991 to 1995, stated that agriculture would receive top priority, and a *People's Daily* editorial in November 1989 noted the precedence of individual interests over those of the collectives. Jiang Zemin, however, addressing the National Farming Conference in 1989, warned of the stagnation of grain and cotton production since 1985, and reaffirmed Chen Yun's dictum – 'There can be no stability without agriculture; without grain there will be chaos.'[46] Once again, it appears that the plan will play the role of guide to the market.

Another important legacy of Mao's economic ideas has been the dismantling of the collectives. The Chinese leaders' official view of Mao's collectivization policies is that they will never be repeated. Simultaneously, however, as the *People's Daily* editorial noted, it continues to insist that co-operation remains a necessary condition of agricultural transformation. By the end of 1984 only 284 communes were left in the country, and 91,171 newly-established township governments had taken over their former role, separating the economic and administrative functions of the commune. The Party was thus enabled to find 100 million jobs for previously non-productive agricultural peasants in semi-industrial co-operatives. This success was built on the rural industrial policy of Mao, with resource – not political – constraints as the only limit on expansion, the change in emphasis from heavy goods to consumer goods reflecting the economies of scale of these rural industries.

The US-trained sociologist, Fei Xiaotong, was led to argue

from this that Chinese industrialization has differed fundamentally from the Western experience, where industrialization grew at the expense of the countryside:

> In contrast, industrialization in socialist China is following an utterly different road. On the basis of a prospering agriculture, the peasants, filled with enthusiasm, run collectively owned township industries. These industries, by assisting, consolidating and promoting the agricultural economy, bring about the simultaneous development of agriculture, sideline occupations and industry. The co-ordinated development of all three sectors of the economy has led to a thriving and prospering countryside. This road to industrialization has been created by the peasants on the basis of their experience in real life. Over the years, millions of peasants have left the land, but not their villages, to enter township industrial enterprises.[47]

The increased specialization of the peasantry, however, led to a new contradiction. After 1986, grain was less attractive for peasants to produce, because prices were kept low by the state in order to feed the urban population. The 1988–9 budget raised the grain price, but only at the cost of higher subsidies on town prices. The state increase in the price of grain encouraged surpluses to be taken to the marketplace, but also led to increased peasant incomes, moving the inter-sectoral terms of trade in favour of agriculture.

This in turn generated more cadre corruption in the cities, and that became one of the main criticisms made by the 1989 protest movement – which found much support in the urban areas because of the effects of inflation on urban wage packets. The Tiananmen Square massacre helped to bring this fundamental policy dilemma into sharper focus for the Party leaders. In 1990, Li Peng, in a speech to a working conference on national production, reaffirmed the open-door policy, adding that domestic and foreign markets must be opened up and that the development of metropolitan and rural markets would continue. The Party was facing difficulties, he added, because the economy was going through structural adjustments.[48]

At the Third Plenum in 1978, the Party had re-examined the Chinese economy amid disquiet about the use of Mao's 'advanced socialism' terminology. The theory used to displace this exaggerated claim was that China was in a stage of 'undeveloped socialism', as expounded by Su Shaozhi and Feng Lanrui. They saw the transition to Communism in three stages: i) the transition from the old society to 'undeveloped socialism', leading to ii) 'developed socialism', and finally into iii) Communism.[49] Although Su has been officially expelled from the Party, this is still the Communist Party's position on the economy, and can be seen in Zhao's theory of the 'primary stage of socialism'. In another sense, 'undeveloped socialism' was the ideological rationalization for decollectivization.

This three-part process, while strongly affected by Marxism, was also influenced by Alvin Toffler's Third Wave theory, which argues that agrarian societies like China represent the first wave; an industrial economy, which China tried to copy from the USSR and more recently from the West and Japan, is the second wave; and now the West and Japan are moving into the third wave, based on the information revolution. The idea that China could avoid the social traumas of the second wave by moving directly into the third wave, was strongly endorsed by Zhao Ziyang and Hu Yaobang. By merely pursuing the second wave, moreover, China would never catch up with the West or Japan. Zhao's target for the year 2000 was for Chinese industrial enterprises to attain the technical levels reached by developed economies in the late 1970s.

In 1986, Deng Xiaoping proposed his vision for the future of the Chinese economy:

During the Cultural Revolution there was a view that poor communism was preferable to rich capitalism. After I resumed office in the central leadership in 1974 and 1975, I criticized that view. Because I refuted that view I was brought down again . . . The main task of socialism is to develop the productive forces, steadily improve the life of the people, and keep increasing the material wealth of society. Therefore, there can be no communism with pauperism, or socialism with pauperism. So to get rich is no sin.[50]

While Deng has refuted Mao's vision of an economic process based on the 'poor and blank' condition of the Chinese people, the importance of Mao's contradictions continue as a motor of change within the economy. Most important, perhaps, is Mao's identification of the peasantry as the vital player in this development process, with its capitalist tendencies now serving hopefully the socialist transformation of China.

In 1989 the People's Republic was the seventh leading country in the world in terms of absolute level of gross national product; sixth in industrial output and power generation; fifth in chemical fibres; fourth in steel output; third in chemical fertilizers; second in coal and cement; and first in clothing. But then China does constitute 22 per cent of mankind. Whether the country could have done 'better' under a capitalist government is a question that is ultimately unanswerable. China's economic development goal is an idealistic one. The economist Lin Guoguang put it succinctly: 'What we emphasize is man's value, a higher level of cultural civilization, and a greater sense of security.'[51] A steadier and less zig-zaggy, less off-the-cuff direction of policy might have paid higher dividends in terms of GNP and the material standard of living, but at the cost of these social goals.

4 Red vs. Expert –
The Question of Intellectuals

John Gurley, the American economist who visited China in the early 1970s, reported:

> Maoists believe that while a principal aim of nations should be to raise the level of material wealth of the population, this should be done only within the context of the development of human beings, encouraging them to realize fully their manifold creative powers. And it should be done only on an egalitarian basis – that is, on the basis that development is not worth much unless everyone rises together; no one is to be left behind, either economically or culturally . . . Development as a trickle-down process is therefore rejected by Maoists.[1]

Mao's emphasis on peasant voluntarism indeed played an important role in the Chinese economy. In the cultural field, this theory was emphasized even more strongly. In 1970, the American writer, Edgar Snow, had a series of interviews with Mao, who stated that of the four titles attributed to him during the Cultural Revolution – Great Teacher, Great Helmsman, Great Supreme Commander and Great Leader – he wished to be remembered by only one, that of Great Teacher.[2] Mao's approach to revolution gives primacy to cultural change. Education should be used to break the traditional patterns of rote learning, scholasticism and meek submission of pupil to teacher. The new culture should be linked to practice, specifically to production, and not separated from class struggle, which was its new driving force. The contradiction involved in this process, however, is over the dichotomy between encouraging a culture that promotes political purity and one that promotes the practical and technical abilities of the individual – between being 'red' and 'expert'.

The traditional Mencian view held by elites in Chinese society was that mental work was superior to manual labour. When the very young Mao was in the Revolutionary Army, fighting against the imperial forces in 1910–11, he refused to carry water. It was beneath his dignity as a student to perform such a menial job. When he arrived at Beijing University later he found himself at the other end of this contemptible game, discriminated against because he was a mere librarian's assistant, and, even worse, from a peasant background.

Peng Pai, Mao's predecessor at the Peasant Movement Training Institute, realized that the cultural baggage of the peasantry and the 'bookish terminology' of the early Communist Party propaganda drives in the countryside had served only to alienate the peasantry. Peng felt alienated by both his own 'bookist' views and speeches, and his dress, and concluded that the peasants' political passivity sprang not simply from grinding material poverty, but more importantly from the way the traditional culture reinforced their sense of hopeless apathy. The solution lay in breaking down the traditional foundations of rural culture, which Mao identified in his *Investigation of the Peasant Movement in Hunan*, in 1927, as the 'four authorities – political, clan, religious and masculine – [which] are the embodiment of the whole feudal-patriarchal system and ideology, and are the four thick ropes binding the Chinese people, particularly the peasants'.[3]

After his defeat in the Autumn Harvest Uprising of 1927, Mao was forced into the countryside and criticized by the Party Central Committee for trying to incorporate bandits into the Red Army. 'In these circumstances,' Mao responded in 1928, 'the only method is to intensify political training, so as to effect a qualitative change in these elements.'[4] The Party, Mao argued, could and should transform men's minds so that they would act as the vanguard of the proletariat. Following the fall of Li Lisan from the Party leadership in 1930, however, the urban-based Central Committee came under the control of Wang Ming, one of the 'returned students' who had been sent to the USSR to be educated in 'correct' Marxist-Leninist theory.

In his speech *Oppose Book Worship* in 1930, Mao criticized his Party colleagues for their strict adherence to dogma.

> If you have not made an investigation of a particular problem, your right to speak on it is suspended. Is this too drastic? Not at all . . . Many inspectors, guerrilla leaders and newly-assigned work cadres like to declare their political opinion the moment they arrive on the scene. After seeing some superficialities, some side issues, they gesticulate and criticize, pointing out mistakes and errors. Such subjective irresponsible talk is most reprehensible. One who talks this way will inevitably ruin the matter and lose mass support.[5]

Mao advised the leaders of the Central Committee in Shanghai to 'stretch your legs, take a walk around your work area, and learn the Confucian way "inquiring into everything".'[6]

In his *On New Democracy* in 1940, Mao explained how important it was to replace the old traditional culture with a new, democratic substitute.

> The new-democratic culture is the anti-imperialist and anti-feudal culture of the broad masses; today it is the culture of the anti-Japanese united front. This culture can be led only by the culture and ideology of the proletariat, by the ideology of communism, and not by the culture and ideology of any other classes. In a word, new-democratic culture is a proletarian-led, anti-imperialist and anti-feudal culture of the broad masses.[7]

Just as the theories of Marx and Lenin had to conform to Chinese conditions in the political sphere, so the new culture also had to be Sinified.

> . . . in applying Marxism in China, Chinese communists must fully and properly integrate the universal truth of Marxism with the concrete practice of the Chinese revolution, or in other words, the universal truth of Marxism must be

combined with specific national characteristics and acquire a definite national form if it is to be useful, and in no circumstances can it be applied subjectively as a mere formula. Marxists who make a fetish of formulas are simply playing the fool with Marxism and the Chinese revolution, and there is no room for them in the ranks of the Chinese revolution. Chinese culture should have its own form, its own national form. National in form and new-democratic in content – such is our culture today.[8]

The Yan'an period between 1937 and 1945, when the Communists were able to rebuild their forces within the second United Front, saw Mao straightening out those 'fools' in the Party who continued to take a dogmatic line in practising Marxism-Leninism. 'Those with book-learning,' he warned at the start of the Rectification Campaign in 1942,

> must develop in the direction of practice; it is only in this way that they will stop being content with books and avoid committing dogmatist errors. Those experienced in work must take up the study of theory and must read seriously; only then will they be able to systematize and synthesize their experience and raise it to the level of theory, only then will they not mistake their partial experience for universal truth and not commit empiricist errors. Dogmatism and empiricism alike are subjectivism, each originating from an opposite pole.[9]

Through this process, the Chinese Communist would be able to practise the theory of Marxism-Leninism among the masses, whose enthusiasm, in turn, would be awakened by the Party cadre. Mao's confidence in the ability of the people to achieve anything, aided by an austere and incorrupt Party, was an important result of the Yan'an era, and has become known in China as the 'Yan'an Spirit'. Mao believed in the revolutionary will of human beings, as a force capable of arbitrarily reshaping the material environment: human beings, not weapons, were the most decisive factor in war. In 1945, in anticipation of a resumption of the civil war, Mao warned Jiang Jieshi that 'The people, and the people alone, are the motive force in the making of world history.'[10] The Communists' swift victory against the Guomindang, backed by the full force of the United States military machine, confirmed Mao's belief in the superiority of people over 'paper tigers'.

To ensure that the people would be the crucial factor in the Chinese revolution, the Chinese Communists had to break the traditional bonds which tied them to the old culture. Yet in promoting Communism in China, they had to ensure that, while pointing the way towards a new and better society, they still employed the language and images of the old culture. In his *On the People's Democratic Dictatorship*, Mao thus used the Chinese word *Datong* to explain the ideal of a Communist society, following Kang Yuwei's usage when challenging the traditional interpretations of Confucianism in the nineteenth century. Confucius had seen *Datong* as China's perfected communal society, once known in an earlier 'golden age', and based on social harmony.[11]

A former Guomindang official gave this commentary on the importance of *Datong* in Chinese culture:

> *Datong* means mutual assistance; everyone has a spirit of mutual assistance and this means that there will be no conflict among the common people and no war between one nation and another . . . Mankind can create this. If everyone has received an education and everyone's point of view is the same, then there will be no disorder, there will be no war . . . Education must be universal, then everyone's knowledge will be about the same and then you can do away with nonsensical bother . . . If everyone's opinions are not the same it can lead to quarrelling and confusion.[12]

While Mao borrowed some Confucian ideas and terminology to explain the Party's ideas, it was still essential for the Communists to break the trinity of ethos, status group and model personality – or Confucianism, gentry and paterfamilias – which were the cultural fetters over the peasants. In his report on the Hunanese peasantry in 1927, Mao described forming peasant associations to enhance the bargaining power of the peasants against local landlords. As for the superstitions which had formed the basis of village culture in China, he had a characteristically blunt comment:

The gods? Worship them by all means. But if you had only Lord Guan and the Goddess of Mercy and no peasant association, could you have overthrown the local tyrants and evil gentry? The gods and goddesses are indeed miserable objects. You have worshipped them for centuries, and they have not overthrown a single one of the local tyrants or evil gentry for you! Now you want to have your rent reduced. Let me ask, how will you go about it? Will you believe in the gods or in the peasant association?[13]

During the initial stages of land reform, the Communists emphasized not just the physical elimination of rural elites, but, more importantly, their psychological disappearance as well. One of the early slogans of the Taiping Rebellion had been *daguan*, or 'smash the officials', and this psychological revolution was furthered by the Communists when land reform came to be carried out. Every act of land reform in the countryside was followed by a drama whereby the landlord expressed his acceptance of defeat by the people by lowering his head (*ditou*), thus forfeiting his position of authority over the people.

Another example was the 'hatting' of the rural elite, a method that was later used against counter-revolutionaries within society and within the Party after 1949. Mao explained it in his report on the Hunanese peasant movement in 1927:

A tall paper-hat is stuck on the head of one of the local tyrants or evil gentry, bearing the words 'Local tyrant so-and-so' or 'So-and-so of the evil gentry'. He is led by a rope and escorted with big crowds in front and behind. Sometimes brass gongs are beaten and flags waved to attract people's attention . . . Anyone who has once been crowned with a tall paper-hat loses face altogether and can never again hold up his head . . . One ingenious peasant association arrested an obnoxious member of the gentry and announced that he was to be crowned that very day. The man turned blue with fear. Then the association decided not to crown him that day. They argued that if he were crowned right away, he would become case-hardened and no longer afraid, and that it would be better to let him go home and crown him some other day. Not knowing when he would be crowned, the man was in daily suspense, unable to sit down or sleep at ease.[14]

The final piece of this evil trinity, the paterfamilias, was one of the strongest social constraints on revolutionary behaviour. Its authority rested on the suppression of women, the majority of whom had to abide by the traditional custom of foot binding. Mao consistently fought against the inferior position of women within society, and ensured that women were treated equally within the Communist Party. The Red Army had the only women's regiment in the country, and one of the first acts of the Communists when they came to power in 1949 was the Marriage Act making 'free choice the basic principle of every marriage'. It aimed to 'put into practice a system of marriage characterized by the freedom to marry for men and women, one wife to one husband, equal rights for men and women, and the protection of the legal rights of wives, sons, and daughters'.[15]

The new trinity which the Communists sought to establish after 1949, in place of Confucianism, the gentry and the paterfamilias, consisted of ideology as the new ethos; the Party as the new status group, deriving authority from ideological purity; and the cadre instead of the paterfamilias, presumed to be both 'red' and 'expert'. The model personality was represented by Mao himself, though increasingly challenged by the emergence of the educated professional.

For Mao, intellectuals represented the biggest challenge to the legitimacy of the Communist ethos. During the Yan'an era, the Communists had attempted to gain as much support as possible for their cause by stressing the importance of uniting China against Japanese aggression, and they succeeded in winning over the majority of urban intellectuals who were stifled by the Guomindang. Intellectuals and artists affronted by the corruption and incompetence of the Jiang Jieshi government flocked to join the Communists in Yan'an – among them the film actress Jiang Qing whom Mao was to marry.

In 1942, in his *Rectify the Party's Style of Work*, Mao issued a warning to these intellectuals.

It is entirely right for us to esteem intellectuals, for without revolutionary intellectuals the revolution cannot triumph. But we all know there are many intellectuals who fancy themelves very learned and assume airs of erudition without realizing that such airs are bad and harmful and hinder their progress. They ought to be aware of the truth that actually many so-called intellectuals are, relatively speaking, most ignorant and the workers and peasants sometimes know more than they do. Here some will say, 'Ha! You are turning things upside down and talking nonsense.' But, comrades, don't get excited; there is some sense in what I am saying.[16]

To Mao, the intellectuals represented as much of a threat to his theories as the dogmatists of the left of the Party or the empiricists on the right. This can be traced back to his desire to break the traditional Mencian view of the difference between mental and manual workers. Yet in 1949 the Party needed all the help it could get from the intellectual classes, and the value put on being 'expert' rose faster than the importance of correct political thinking. Mao was worried lest the contradiction between red and expert increasingly divide the elites within society, leading to a juxtaposition of the Chinese Communist Party composed largely of workers and peasants, and an intelligentsia made up of the most educated people in society – the Party masters of ideology, the intellectuals controlling technology.

During the early 1950s, therefore, many intellectuals were enrolled into the Party, in order to ensure their allegiance and balance the Party's class make-up. The intellectuals bore the main brunt of early political campaigns – the '3-Antis' and '5-Antis' – against the bourgeoisie and the state bureaucracy, as the Communists tested their loyalty to the new government. Their increased expertise encouraged their individualism and their mental rejection of theories based on mass egalitarianism.

In 1957, a year after the Party announced the end of classes in society at the Eighth Congress, Mao stated that 'in the eyes of some of these [intellectuals], there is no need to be concerned about politics, about the future of the fatherland, about the ideals of humanity'.[17] Mao complained that a 'change in world-view is a basic transformation; we still cannot say that the majority of intellectuals have completed this transformation'.[18]

In February 1957, Mao outlined the major contradictions that remained within this classless society, in his *On the Question of Correctly Resolving Contradictions Among the People*.

> Under present conditions, the so-called contradictions among the people include contradictions within the working class, within the peasantry, within the intellectuals; contradictions between the working class and the peasant classes; contradictions of workers and peasants with the intellectuals; contradictions of the working class and other toiling people with the national bourgeoisie class; contradictions within the national bourgeoisie class, and so on. Our government truly is a government that serves the people. These contradictions include contradictions of state interest and collective interest with individual interest, the contradiction of democracy and centralism, the contradiction of leader and led, the contradiction of bureaucratism of some workers in state agencies with the masses. This is also a contradiction among the people. In general, contradictions among the people are contradictions on a foundation of basic harmony of the people's interests.[19]

Mao was convinced that, in contradistinction to the rise of 'counter-revolutionaries' in Hungary in 1956, the Chinese people understood the limits of their freedom. 'Under democratic centralism,' he remarked, 'the people enjoy a wide measure of democracy and freedom, but at the same time they have to keep themselves within the bounds of socialist discipline. All this is well understood by the masses of the people.'[20] In the spring of 1957, the Party issued a call to 'let a hundred flowers bloom'. Deng Xiaoping supported the China Youth Special 'Hot Pepper' editions, which published criticisms of the Party's policies, and pronounced to intellectuals that, 'if you dare not criticize, dare not speak out just because the criticism contains some defects, then you'll return to the lifeless silence of the past. That kind of silent frustration is not good.'[21]

The Hundred Flowers policy was not a programme of liberalization, but was intended to show that Marxism, being the only true form of thought, would eventually triumph over all others, thereby educating non-Communist intellectuals and writers, and transforming them into socialist intellectuals. The criticisms of non-Marxists would also make Marxists re-examine their own views. 'Correct ideas,' Mao stated, 'if pampered in hothouses without exposure to the elements or immunization against disease, will not win out against wrong ones.'[22]

Critics of the government, however, were not merely critical of particular abuses of power, but questioned the very legitimacy of the Communist Party's monopoly of power and ideology. A Democracy Square flourished at Beijing University, and one student, Lin Xiling, soon became the target of Party criticism after stating:

> The problem of Stalin is not the problem of Stalin the individual; the problem of Stalin could only arise in a country like the Soviet Union, because in the past it had been a feudal, imperialistic nation. China is the same, for there is no tradition of bourgeois democracy . . . I hold that the socialism we now have is not genuine socialism, or that if it is, our socialism is not typical. Genuine socialism should be very democratic, but ours is undemocratic. I venture to say that our society is a socialist one erected on a feudal foundation; it is not typical socialism, and we must struggle for genuine socialism.[23]

A worried Mao then launched a fierce Anti-Rightist Campaign, during which 15–40 per cent of the leaders of the eight official democratic parties and 2–3 per cent of Party members were imprisoned. The emphasis was switched to socialist discipline, and Mao recommended that these 'rightist elements' should be sent to the countryside to experience hard labour, which was doubtless a useful experience for intellectuals who harboured the traditional profound contempt for manual work, but was medically dangerous and very humiliating for many. Labelled as 'counter-revolutionaries' within the classless society, these intellectuals, and their children, were stigmatized in every political campaign that followed.

In Mao's *On the Ten Great Relationships* in 1957, he asked, 'What harm is there in not executing people? Those amenable to labour reform should go and do labour reform, so that rubbish can be transformed into something useful. Besides, people's heads are not like leeks. When you cut them off, they will not grow again. If you cut off a head wrongly, there is no way of rectifying the mistake even if you want to.'[24] While the intellectuals were generally spared the brutality and liquidation which the rural elites, and the working classes, were subjected to, the Party used them as objects of vilification. In traditional Chinese culture, the intellectuals had represented authority, locked away behind closed doors, and unanswerable to the masses. Under the Communists the intellectuals were directly responsible to the masses, who were represented by the Party itself.

Two months after the launch of the Anti-Rightist Campaign, the Party inaugurated a socialist education movement to ensure that these disparate views voiced by the intellectuals would not be accepted by the people as a whole. This was a pattern that would be repeated after every period of political 'liberalization'. In 1949 Mao had acknowledged that 'the serious problem is the education of the peasantry', because of their unproletarian political consciousness. In 1956 he mentioned for the first time, and at great length, the disadvantages for China arising out of its semi-colonial past and economic backwardness, and only then suggested that this 'poverty and blankness' had a positive side.

By 1958, following the Hundred Flowers Movement, Mao saw only advantages in the purity and revolutionary zeal which could be derived from China's backwardness. At the Eighth Party Congress in that year he stated:

Apart from their other characteristics, China's 600 million people have two remarkable peculiarities; they are, first of all, poor, and secondly blank. That may seem like a bad thing, but it is really a good thing. Poor people want change, want to do things, want revolution. A clean sheet of paper has no blotches, and so the newest and most beautiful words can be written on it, the newest and most beautiful pictures can be painted on it.[25]

The new words and pictures, of course, were the correct political application of Marx and Lenin to China, or the thought of Mao Zedong. This would replace the culture of traditional China, which still led intellectuals to interpret Chinese society wrongly, and to criticize the Party as they had done during the Hundred Flowers Movement.

The new culture was epitomized in the Great Leap Forward of that year, in the 'three-unification movement', which aimed to resolve the contradictions within society which Mao had listed in the previous year. The result would be the unity of these contradictions, in that each class was expected, in effect, to become the other – workers becoming technicians, technicians becoming workers, and both sharing leadership with the cadres. Workers were also expected to become generalists, because of the over-emphasis on specialists during the First Five Year Plan. This, it was argued, would aid the development process, because only a few months' training was needed to turn a peasant into a jack-of-all-trades, while it took years of study before an intellectual could specialize in anything.

Because human beings were malleable, social mobilization could, Mao believed, motivate them to work better than material incentives could. Wages were dispensed with during the Great Leap and replaced by 'distribution'. This meant that the worker or peasant in the commune would be supplied with a sum of money and goods needed to support his or her family, with cash wages reduced to the function of pocket money. The Communist policy was to appeal to the masses, not through material rewards or techniques, but through spiritual values transmitted by ideology.[26]

In his *Das Kapital*, Marx states:

No matter what social form production takes, labour and the means of production are factors in production. In the event that they are cut off from each other, both of them are still potential factors in production. If anything is to be produced, they must always be brought together. The particular method or form of their union is what distinguishes the social structure of each different economic era.[27]

The fact that the Chinese people were poor and therefore revolutionary tends to bear Marx out. But the working class are the most revolutionary class only because of their relationship with the modes of production, not because of their material (non)wealth. The idea, however, that 'blankness' is also a revolutionary attribute is strictly a Maoist gloss on Marx.

Just as Marx had identified the working class as the only possible leaders of the revolution, because of their potential Promethean thrust, so he also looked to them as the bedrock of the new socialist culture. For Mao, however, this implied that Western workers were superior not only to their Asian counterparts, but also to the quintessence of the Chinese revolution, the peasantry. Mao's clash with the post-Stalinist leaders in the Soviet Union after 1956 prompted him to elevate the 'poor and blank' attributes of the Chinese peasantry into a revolutionary virtue, which would not distract the Chinese Party from the socialist path. While they did not have the technical competence and economic development of the USSR, China's peasants were unafflicted by the maladies of crass materialism, and could be relied upon to aid the development of socialism. During the early years of the Cultural Revolution, the emphasis was on learning from the peasants, reflecting, in Schram's felicitous phrasing, 'Mao's resolve to struggle not only against the Confucian prejudice regarding the superiority of mental over manual workers, but also against the Marxist prejudice regarding the superiority of the worker over the peasant'.[28]

Increasingly after 1958, Mao questioned traditional Chinese elitism in education – the exaggerated reverence for scholars and intellectuals – just as he called into question the elitism of the Leninist mystique of the Party as the locus of political consciousness. He made short work of learning Marxism by rote: 'We shouldn't read too many books. We should read Marxist books, but not too many of them either. It will be enough to read a few dozen. If we read too many we can . . . become bookworms, dogmatists, revisionists . . .'[29] Better by far to reaffirm class struggle, which became a major slogan of the Tenth Plenum of the Central Committee in 1962. 'Class struggle is your most important subject,' Mao told his student nephew in 1964. 'Only when you have completed such a course of political training (by going to factories and the countryside) can I consider you a university graduate . . . If you don't even know about the class struggle, how can you be regarded as a university graduate?'[30]

But the real reason for the continuing need for class struggle lay within the Party itself. After 1959, a system of two-line leadership had been established, with the first line (Liu Shaoqi, Deng Xiaoping and Zhou Enlai) running day-to-day affairs, and the second line (Mao Zedong) ensuring that the correct political decisions were made. The example of the post-Stalinist leaders in the Soviet Union, who were increasingly strafed by the Chinese Communists for their revisionist theories, heightened Mao's fears lest the Party lose its revolutionary élan. In 1963, a year before the launch of the Socialist Education Movement, Mao sent a warning to his Party colleagues in an article entitled *On Khrushchev's Phoney Communism and Its Historical Lessons for the World*, justifying the need for such campaigns:

If, in the absence of these movements, the landlords, rich peasants, counter-revolutionaries, bad elements and ogres of all kinds were allowed to crawl out, while our cadres were to shut their eyes to all this and in many cases fail even to differentiate between the enemy and ourselves, but were to collaborate with the enemy and were corrupted, divided and demoralized by him, if our cadres were thus pulled out or the enemy were able to sneak in, and if many of our workers, peasants and intellectuals were left defenceless against both the soft and the hard tactics of the enemy, then it would not take long, perhaps only several years or a decade, or several decades at most, before a counter-revolutionary restoration on a national scale inevitably occurred, the Marxist-Leninist party would undoubtedly become a revisionist party or a fascist party, and the whole of China would change its colour.[31]

In attacking the Party, Mao turned first to the army in an attempt to recreate the 'Yan'an Spirit' which had benefited the movement so much during the civil war. The militarily able, but politically sycophantic Lin Biao had been appointed Minister of Defence after Peng Dehuai had criticized Mao at the Lushan Plenum in 1959, following the débâcle of the Great Leap. In 1963 a propaganda campaign began extolling the life story of a former People's Liberation Army soldier called Lei Feng, who had been orphaned during the civil war and had found a new 'family' in the People's Republic, where he performed numerous feats of public service. In an article in *China Youth* in May 1963, Hu Yaobang, the leader of the Central Committee of the Youth League, noted that 'looking through Lei Feng's diary we can discover one point that is extremely enlightening, his spirit of self-examination, self-criticism and self-motivation.'[32]

Simultaneously, Jiang Qing, Mao's wife and a former actress in Shanghai, began attacking various cultural productions for not reflecting the Party's views. Speaking about the spread of traditional opera in China in the early 1960s, she objected that, 'They never put on stage the rich achievements of our people, or the Long March, or the Red Army, or the Anti-Japanese War. They never put on all these heroic things. Films had the same problem. In 1962 I talked about it with four ministers or deputies from propaganda and culture, but they wouldn't listen to me.'[33]

The Socialist Education Movement in 1964 failed, however, to inspire the Party in the way that Mao desired, and so, two years later, he launched the Great Proletarian Cultural Revolution, in a last attempt to instil a sense of revolutionary enthusiasm into the youth of the country. Mao had given a speech in March 1958 entitled *Against Blind Faith in Learning*, setting out his aims in the educational field.

Of course some things can be learnt at school; I don't propose to close all the schools. What I mean is that it is not absolutely necessary to attend school. The main thing is whether your direction is correct or not and whether you come to grips with your studies. Learning has to be grasped. As soon as they had grasped the truth the young founders of new schools embarked on discoveries, scorning the old fogeys. Then those with learning oppressed them. Isn't that what history is like? When we started to make revolution, we were twenty-year-old boys, while the rulers of that time, like Yuan Shikai and Duan Qijui, were old and experienced. They had more learning, but we had more truth.[34]

In 1967, a year after the launch of the Cultural Revolution, the *Red Flag* stated: 'All cultural movements in contemporary Chinese history have begun with student movements and [have] led to the worker and peasant movements, to the integration of revolutionary intellectuals with the worker-peasant masses. This is an objective law . . . In 1967, China's Great Proletarian Cultural Revolution will continue to develop in line with this objective law.'[35] Thus, just as the Chinese Communist Party had sprung from the dissenting voices of the May 4 Movement in 1919, so the post-Cultural Revolutionary Party would be infected by the spirit of youthful élan, over the experience and learning of the Party elders. By promoting the superiority of the young over the old, Mao was of course conceding that one of the three mainstays of the old culture had yet to be dismantled – that of filial loyalty.

On the eve of the Cultural Revolution, Mao had also turned conventional Marxist theory on its head, by indicating to his nephew, Mao Yuanxin, which class held this revolutionary élan:

Formerly, I was a principal of a primary school, and a teacher in a middle school. I am also a member of the central committee, and was once a department chief for the Guomindang. But when I went to rural areas and spent some time with peasants, I was deeply struck by how many things they knew. I realized their knowledge was wide and I was no match for them, but should learn from them.[36]

Following the near-anarchy of the first two years of the campaign, Mao launched the 'Back to the Countryside Movement' in December 1968. 'It is very necessary,' he remarked, 'for educated young people to go to the countryside to be re-educated by the poor and lower-middle peasants. Cadres and other people in the cities should be persuaded to send their sons and daughters who have finished junior or senior middle school, college or university to the countryside.'[37] Between 1968 and 1976, 12 million students were sent to the countryside, as Mao reasserted his belief in the popular will over the orthodox Marxist-Leninist viewpoint that the peasantry should be penetrated with technical knowledge and the discipline of the working class.

While challenging the Confucian concept of the inferiority of the younger generation to their elders, and the Marxist view of the unrivalled Promethean spirit of the working class, Mao also slammed the traditional methods of teaching in China, hoping to liquidate the traditional breeding grounds of scholar-bureaucratism. While praising Confucius for his acknowledgement of the suffering of the masses, Mao attacked the traditional system of rote learning, and emphasized the need for pupils to work out their own problems. 'In the past,' Mao confided to his nephew,

> when I was teaching at Kangda, I used to distribute lecture notes to my students in advance. I only talked for thirty minutes, and let the students themselves do their own study; afterwards the students would ask questions and the teacher would answer. With university students, especially the senior students, the main thing is to let them study and work out problems. What is the point of talking so much?[38]

By belittling the traditional reliance on rote learning in education, Mao was implicitly scourging the dogmatists who carried on the tradition by the rote learning of Marxism. Education should combine Marxist theory with Chinese practice, and by promoting his own interpretations of Marxism-Leninism, Mao was showing how this revolutionary spirit could be infused into a new Chinese culture. Society was to be the biggest university of the future.

One Red Guard confirmed that, 'When I went to university, we former Red Guards met to exchange our experiences. We agreed that our stay with the people in the country had taught us the value of things – and of life itself.' Another former Red Guard, Liu Guokai, reported that the Cultural Revolution 'widened people's horizons. They learnt so many things hitherto unknown to them. They began to think and analyse.' The final result, however, was that after 'the onslaughts of the Cultural Revolution, the existing regime lost its former holy lustre. Cadres were unmasked and lost their former prestige, which was built upon deceit, whitewash and administrative order . . .'[39] Mao launched the Cultural Revolution to re-create the spirit of Yan'an which had given the Chinese Communist Party its revolutionary legitimacy, but the Party came out of the Cultural Revolution with its revolutionary credibility in tatters.

The method chosen by Mao to free the Chinese people of their centuries-old passivity towards authority was through aggression, controlled by a 'correct' line of thinking and action. But there were problems with 'hate psychology'. During the civil war period, and until the Party announced the end of classes in Chinese society in 1956, there were easily identifiable enemies which the Party promoted for people to hate – for example, the landlords during the land reform campaign. Bureaucratic tendencies continued to exist after 1956, not only among intellectuals, as the Hundred Flowers Movement showed, but also within the Party itself. By promoting Party cadres, and even Party leaders, as objects for vilification, Mao hoped to create a culture in which the masses would feel free to criticize authority.

The 'correct' line of thinking mirrored the process which Mao and his colleagues had gone through since 1919, resting ultimately on the priority of struggling against 'bourgeois thought'. However, by making the Party lose face before the masses, Mao forfeited his chance of uniting the two contradictions, red and expert. Instead, he created a new contradiction, in which the masses are more politically conscious without becoming necessarily more red, while the Party, having lost its public prestige, has to fall back on traditional Chinese elites, espousing expertness as a political and economic expediency. One example of the increased consciousness of the Chinese people has come from China-watchers in Hong Kong who report that interviewing Chinese refugees who flee to the British colony is now immensely rewarding because 'first, these refugees, both intellectual and non-intellectual, are articulate; and second, they have a habit of analysing everything'.[40]

By promoting class struggle during the Cultural Revolution as the only possible solution to the problems inherent in the traditional culture, Mao was referring back to his report on the Hunanese peasants in 1927, when he gave his most famous statement on revolution.

A revolution is not the same as inviting people to dinner or writing an essay or painting a picture or embroidering a flower; it cannot be anything so refined, so calm and gentle, or so 'mild, kind, courteous, restrained and magnanimous' [the classical Confucian virtues]. A revolution is an uprising, an act of violence whereby one class overthrows the authority of another . . . To right a wrong it is necessary to exceed the proper limit; the wrong cannot be righted without doing so . . .[41]

Mao's major contribution to the theory and practice of revolution was extreme voluntarism. He preferred a man who wills to a man who knows.

Men are not the slaves of objective reality. Provided only that men's consciousness be in conformity with the objective laws of the development of things, the subjective activity of the popular masses can manifest itself in full measure, overcome all difficulties, create the necessary conditions, and carry forward the revolution. In this sense, the subjective creates the objective.[42]

The contradiction between 'red' and 'expert' continued in China after Mao's death. The central theme of the new agricultural policies in 1979 was the need to combat 'egalitarianism', by implementing a policy of 'from each according to his ability; to each according to his work'. Not that the Chinese leaders have dispensed entirely with Mao's methods for creating a new culture. In a speech in 1983 to the Congress of Art Workers, Deng Xiaoping echoed Mao's *Talks at the Yan'an Forum on Literature and Art* of 1942:

> It is our hope that more and more comrades among literary and art workers will become real engineers who can rebuild the human soul. In order to educate the people, they should first be educated. In order to provide the people with mental food, they themselves must first absorb nourishment. Then who will educate literary and art workers? The Marxist answer can only be: the people.[43]

But the cult of Lei Feng was replaced by the 'cult of the entrepreneur' for most of the 1980s.

The Party's relationship with intellectuals remains tense. During the Cultural Revolution, the intellectuals were branded the 'stinking Number Nine' – the ninth category of social enemy after the landlords, rich peasants, counter-revolutionaries, bad elements, rightists, renegades, enemy agents and capitalist roaders. In an apparent recognition of the fact that the role of the intellectuals was crucial to China's development, Mao had confessed in 1975 that 'we can't do without Number Nine'. After his death, and the fall of the Gang of Four, China became an increasingly technocratic society. Hu Yaobang, the former General Secretary, argued that in a socialist society intellectuals had already become part of the working class, complaining that 'Red is red, and expert is expert. Why make so much fuss of it!'[44]

Deng's emphasis on economic modernization has meant more experts working at the policy initiation stage – at jobs which used to be reserved for those whose political line was correct, no matter if someone more able were available. This has created a complex relationship between intellectuals seeking to participate in the policy process and the state, whereby political authorities prefer to solicit the views of intellectuals individually, thus creating a system of patronage. For example,

Zhao Ziyang and Wan Li actively encouraged and supported the 'Study Group on Problems of Chinese Rural Development', but when Zhao fell from power in 1989, the group lost its political backing.

The intellectuals have been allowed more freedom under Deng than under Mao, but the political boundaries of criticism still remain. In 1979, Deng promoted the Democracy Wall movement to assist his consolidation of power within the Party, but as soon as the protesters began demanding democracy as the fifth modernization, the wall was closed. The right to display wall posters, one of the 'four great freedoms' (speaking out freely, airing one's views fully, writing big-character posters and holding great debates) which Mao had first proposed in 1957, and which had been written into the Constitution in 1978, was curtailed by the National People's Conference the following year.

In 1985, Deng promoted a second Hundred Flowers Movement, asking intellectuals to air their grievances against the Party. Some called for more human rights or more scientific and artistic freedom, and the astro-physicist Fang Lizhi even argued that 'intellectuals, who own and create information and knowledge, are the most dynamic component of the productive forces', propelling his fellow-intellectuals into the vanguard role of the proletariat.[45] Once again there was a backlash Anti-Rightist campaign, not as brutal as the 1958 version, but carried out by the same judge and jury – Deng Xiaoping and Peng Zhen.

Towards the end of the 1980s, intellectuals began to reassert their autonomy from political leaders, through such organizations as the Sitong Development Research Institute and other non-governmental institutes, giving them a freedom and influence unknown since 1949. The case of the *World Economic Herald*, however, shows the fragile nature of this freedom. In April 1989 the Shanghai Party Committee, headed at that time by Jiang Zemin, banned the first issue of this quasi-governmental newspaper and dismissed its editor Qin Benli, installing a 'rectification leading small group' to ensure the maintenance of the correct line in the paper. Although Shanghai and Beijing intellectuals protested that the Shanghai Party did not have the authority to close down the paper and demanded Qin's reinstatement, the *World Economic Herald* was suspended from publication in May 1989.

The contradiction between 'red' and 'expert' still exists within Chinese society today, as a tool for political control over the intellectuals and the masses. Following the massacre in Beijing in June 1989, the Party authorities announced that, for the first time in recent years, high-school students in Beijing would be sent to a military camp for a month of light-weapons training, formation drill and political indoctrination. The distrust with which the present leaders view the masses has persuaded them to revert to the famous sloganeering of the Cultural Revolution – of 'Learning from the People's Liberation Army' and following the example of Lei Feng. Premier Li Peng, in a speech in January 1990, stated that the ideal legal training for judges would make them 'effective in understanding and settling issues in keeping with the views of Marxism-Leninism-Mao Zedong Thought. Priority should be given to political quality in the training of justice officials.'[46] The most nostalgic of these echoes of Mao's theories came in 1990 from the veteran Peng Zhen, one of the original targets of the Cultural Revolution, when he regretted that 'things are much more numerous and ideas are much more chaotic' than they used to be, and proposed a return to the Spirit of Yan'an.[47]

In the 1980s the Communist Party's reliance on coercion and arbitrary arrest because of widespread unpopularity rendered the formerly stigmatic label of 'counter-revolutionary' more socially acceptable. As Wei Jingsheng, the most famous of the Democracy Wall activists, stated at his trial in October 1979: 'The fate of Marxism is like many religions in history: after the second and third generations its revolutionary essence is abstracted and its theoretical ideals are used to deceive the people.'[48] Class struggle and criticism of authorities still persist, as Mao would have wished. Su Shaozhi, the neo-Marxist professor, recognized that, 'Theoretical workers must have real courage and boldness of vision, and must ponder questions independently rather than mechanically following the instructions of higher authorities and books. They must not be afraid of being regarded as advocates of "unorthodox opinions".

Many such opinions were later proved correct through scientific experiments.'[49]

Ultimately, however, the political line of the Party has been upheld, and Mao's dream of creating a new socialist human being, full of political enthusiasm and technical ability, has not materialized, although the possibility of dissent is still there within the Marxist-Leninist rhetoric. As Tan Zhenlin, then Minister of Agriculture, protested to Mao during a Cultural Revolution struggle meeting in 1967,

> The masses, it's always the masses, what about Party leadership? It's all day long without the Party, the masses liberating themselves, educating themselves, making revolution. What's it all about? It's metaphysics! Your aim is just to overthrow the old cadres and clean them out one by one. Once you've fixed all the old cadres, forty years of revolution will be smashed like a broken family.[50]

5 *Idealism vs. Realpolitik* – The Question of the Third World

The victory of the Chinese Communist Party in 1949 was greeted with enthusiasm by revolutionary leaders in many colonial and semi-colonial countries. Against all the odds, the Chinese Communists, after twenty-two years of civil war and with no substantial help from any foreign power, defeated the American-backed forces of the Guomindang. Many radicals supposed that the Chinese lesson would have relevance for the rest of the Third World.

Although his contacts with foreign revolutionary leaders before 1949 were negligible, Mao Zedong was well aware of the symbolic international importance of his party's victory. As early as 1936, in an interview with Edgar Snow, he had claimed that: 'The Chinese revolution is a key factor in the world situation . . . When the Chinese revolution comes into full power, the masses of many colonial countries will follow the example of China and win a similar victory of their own.'[1]

Nine years later, at the so-called Congress of Victors in Yan'an, Liu Shaoqi offered this piece of advice to prospective revolutionary leaders of the Third World: 'The thought of Mao Zedong . . . will make great and useful contributions to the struggle for the emancipation of the peoples of all countries in general, and of the peoples of the East in particular.'[2]

The Chinese leaders were, however, slow to formulate a distinct role for themselves in the Third World, or to follow up theory with practical measures. In 1949 Mao had proclaimed that China would 'lean to one side' in its relations with the international community, while basing its foreign relations on 'the principles of equality, mutual benefit, and mutual respect for territorial integrity and sovereignty'. Liu Shaoqi, speaking at the World Federation of Trade Unions in Beijing in November, reaffirmed his earlier statement about the applicability of the Chinese experience: 'The way which has been followed by the Chinese people . . . is the way which should be followed by the peoples of many colonial and semi-colonial countries in their struggle for national independence and people's democracy.'[3]

The outbreak of the Korean War in 1950, and the decision by the Central Committee to send Chinese 'Volunteers' to fight alongside the North Koreans, put an early limit on the possibilities of Chinese involvement in the Third World. All available resources had to be funnelled into the war. China's isolation in international affairs, and her leaders' inexperience in international diplomacy, in any case hampered the task of promoting a Chinese model of revolution.

Indeed the first five years of the new government proved to be a period of moderation in foreign policy. China followed a line of 'peaceful co-existence' culminating in Zhou Enlai's triumphal performance at the Bandung Conference of Afro-Asian countries in 1955 which echoed his moralistic stance at the Korean Armistice talks two years earlier. Nehru's role in the protracted Korean War armistice talks had consolidated his already high prestige in the Third World, yet at Bandung he accepted Zhou on an equal footing – as the two principal representatives of the non-European world, divided by ideology but united by their Asianness.

Zhou's *tour de force* in exuding sweet reasonableness at Bandung, and his joint formulation with Nehru of the five principles of peaceful co-existence (two of which were faithfully reproduced from Mao's foreign-relations speech of June 1949), helped to allay Asian anxiety about China's potential expansionism. In 1939 Mao had been explicit in cataloguing the conquests by foreign imperialists of 'a large number of states tributary to China, as well as a part of her own territory. Japan appropriated Korea, Taiwan, the Ryukyu islands, the Pescadores and Port Arthur; England took Burma, Bhutan, Nepal and Hongkong; France seized Annam; even a miserable little country like Portugal took Macau from us . . .'[4]

By the 1950s, however, the Chinese Communists were keen to stress their rejection of their ancestors' imperialist past and to reassure their neighbours that they did not harbour any expansionist tendencies. Although China has been involved in two border wars in the past forty years, it has never attempted to annex any of these formerly tributary states. But the historical fear of Chinese intentions, along with the success of so many Asian countries in winning independence largely without violence (through a peaceful transition from colonial powers to local politicians) and the division of most of Asia into Cold War alignments, all served to handicap the chances of Chinese-style revolutions in Asia. Instead, following the Bandung Conference, China turned its attention to Africa.

The Chinese encounter with Africa goes back to the beginning of the fifteenth century, when Admiral Zheng He landed on the East African coast and trading started between China and Africa. By the time the Chinese Communists came to power, Africa was parcelled out among the European colonial powers, and nascent independence movements had only just begun to take the steps towards political freedom which their Asian counterparts mostly took for granted. The Chinese message, of violent revolutionary upheaval against foreign domination, struck an immediate chord with many African revolutionaries.

Zhou's oratory at the Bandung Conference of Afro-Asian countries in 1955 highlighted these resonances between Chinese and African experience. It was also at Bandung that Zhou met the figurehead of African independence hopes, President Abdul Nasser of Egypt. Nasser recognized the Beijing government in 1956, a move which brought him into direct conflict with the US and helped to precipitate the Suez crisis. In the following year China was accorded a position of great prestige in the Afro-Asian People's Solidarity Organization, from which it was able to cultivate relations with independence movements along the length and breadth of the African continent.

At this time Zhou was still recognizing that the peoples of many Asian and African countries had 'embarked on the road of independence and development under the leadership of the nationalists'.[5] This mirrored the orthodox Marxist-Leninist standpoint of the Soviet leaders, who argued that African Communists should ally themselves with left-wing nationalist parties. By striking at the 'safe rear' of colonialism, African Communists would facilitate the revolution in the capitalist countries.

In 1958, however, this policy of a 'united front from above' was superseded by the 'united front from below', through the promotion of revolution by opposition forces. Mao was increasingly distrustful of Nasser and Nehru, regarding them as bourgeois, unreliable in opposing imperialism, and potentially pro-Soviet. Nasser's formation of a United Arab Republic in 1958 through a union with Syria, designed to check the rise of the Syrian Communists, appeared to epitomize the dangers of trusting nationalist rulers in the struggle against imperialism. It was a lesson which the Chinese Communists had learnt from their own experiences in Shanghai in 1927.

As relations with Nasser became strained, the Chinese leaders turned their attention to other parts of Africa. Initially the Chinese played out a missionary role, hoping to share their experiences of fighting against imperialism with Africans who might be interested in them, not merely because they were Communists, but because they had managed to break with the West and won independence, and had then gone on to hold their own against the US in Korea for three years.

The Chinese, adroitly led by Premier and Foreign Minister Zhou Enlai, cultivated these relationships with skill, treating the African leaders better, and less patronizingly, than the Europeans had ever done. In the late 1950s many African revolutionaries were invited to Beijing, to be given a hero's welcome. Walter Sisulu, of the African National Congress, went to Beijing as early as 1953, where he felt he had been treated, for the first time in his life, 'as a dignified human being'. Others were encouraged by the words of the great African revolutionary hero, Dubois: 'China is the flesh of your flesh and blood of your blood'.[6]

In 1963 Zhou Enlai embarked on a tour of Africa, carefully selecting countries which had historical links with China through Admiral Zheng He's voyage in the fifteenth century. China and Africa, he maintained, had been brought back together again by their common experience of the oppressive Western imperialism. In another, more famous, statement, Zhou declared that 'revolutionary prospects are excellent throughout the African continent'.[7]

Although many Westerners took this to mean that China

was about to embark on a crusade of revolution throughout Africa, Zhou was simply highlighting the fact that because many African countries were still not independent, they were fighting for their freedom, while those that *were* independent were still potentially revolutionary because of the residue of cultural and economic imperialism which had been left behind by the Europeans. It was left ambiguous how far Zhou meant also to observe the makings of indigenous revolution against indigenous feudal or semi-feudal forces which sometimes filled the power vacuum in Africa after European rule had crumbled.

As the split between China and the Soviet Union widened, and revolutionary parties in the West moved towards democratic revolution, so Mao's views on where the world revolution would succeed matured. An editorial in the *People's Daily* in 1963, following the theory of D.N. Aidit, the leader of the Indonesian Communist Party, stated that: 'Today the national liberation revolutions in Asia, Africa and Latin America are the most important forces dealing imperialism direct blows. The contradictions of the world are concentrated in Asia, Africa and Latin America.'[8] Mao neatly reversed Lenin's theory of striking against the 'safe rear' of imperialism, by stating that 'the rear has become the front'.

Mao further emphasized China's links with Africa by proclaiming that the countries lying between the socialist and imperialist camps belonged to the world countryside, whence the revolution would eventually move to the cities of the West. But, unlike its Soviet counterpart, the main thrust of the Chinese message was not that potential African revolutionaries had to follow the Chinese experiences literally, but that they had the right to take their own initiatives. If they wanted support from the Chinese they only had to ask for it. But the Chinese would not rigidly impose their doctrines on the Africans, as the Soviets had attempted to do to the Chinese Communists during the 1920s and 1930s.

Every resistance movement in Africa was at some stage trained by the Chinese: the African National Congress and Pan-Africanist Congress from South Africa; the South West African People's Organization (SWAPO) in Namibia; the Zimbabwe African People's Union (ZAPU), and, later, the breakaway faction led by Robert Mugabe, the Zimbabwe African National Union (ZANU); the Popular Movement for the Liberation of Angola (MPLA) and the Front for Liberation of Mozambique (FRELIMO). They were given military hardware, for example, the Chinese version of the AK-47 Kalashnikov, as well as funds, food and medicine.

Initially this military training took place in Nanjing, but that was not terribly practical and training camps were later established in Ghana and Tanzania. Here Chinese instructors applied Maoist guerrilla doctrines by comparing them with earlier African struggles against imperialism, like the Zulu Chief Shaka's campaigns against the British in the nineteenth century. The basic tenet which the Chinese passed on was the importance of winning local peasant support. One way to achieve this was through the use of simplistic and easily understandable political phrases, of which Maoism was full, and which were adapted to African conditions. The importance of army discipline was also emphasized to win over peasant support.

For many African revolutionary leaders, however, the emphasis on peasant support was irrelevant. South Africa was highly urbanized, and the major political struggles were taking place within the industrialized sectors of the South African economy rather than on the land which was mostly owned by white farmers. In Guinea there was no historical precedent for a revolutionary peasantry. Yet, even in these areas the Chinese message worked in a sense, as it encouraged African initiatives suited to African conditions.

One case where Mao's belief in the peasantry was taken seriously and followed with success occurred in Zimbabwe. ZANU, which had split from Joshua Nkomo's ZAPU movement, fought a series of disastrous campaigns against the Rhodesian Army. From 1966 to 1970, under the supervision of 'Comrade Li' at Tanzanian camps, ZANU troops were imbued with Maoist doctrines about the necessity of winning over the support of the peasantry through discipline and honesty. In December 1972 ZANU began a new campaign, slowly and methodically moving through the countryside, and winning over the villages indeed through education and raising the level of political consciousness. By 1979 ZANU controlled two-thirds of the countryside – enabling Robert Mugabe to stake his claim as President of the newly independent republic in 1980.

Those countries in Africa which had already achieved independence in the early 1960s, but which Zhou appeared to target for further revolutionary upheaval in his 1963 speech, had less time for the Chinese, for a number of reasons. First, they shied away from the rigidity of Communist ideology, having only just won their own political freedom from the West. Second, China's own development pattern of social regimentation underestimated the importance of the family unit in African society. Third, many African leaders rejected the revolutionary nature of Chinese Communism, preferring peaceful change and stability.

Even so, Zhou's high visibility and diplomatic flair helped to overcome to some extent these negative images of China in Africa. Kwame Nkrumah in Ghana, Julius Nyerere in Tanzania and Kenneth Kaunda in Zambia all took pieces of the Maoist doctrine and applied them in their own countries. In Tanzania, Nyerere blended Chinese communization with the traditional African concept of *ujamaa*, or the collective strength of the village. He attempted to narrow the gap between the peasantry and the urban elite through compulsory work in the *ujamaa*, enlisting the army to work alongside the peasants and promoting a 'leadership code' of frugality.

These examples were the essence of Zhou's idea that China should act only as a point of reference for African revolutionary leaders. China had shown that it could hold its own against the might of the imperialist powers, while promoting a development path based on the mobilization of human beings in place of scarce machinery. More importantly, perhaps, as Philip Snow put it in *The Star Raft*: 'Brimful of confidence in the aftermath of their own revolutionary triumph, the Chinese Communists succeeded to a significant extent in passing that confidence on.'[9]

Apparently oblivious to the apprehensions of many conservative African leaders, who shared the European colonialists' fear of Communist domination, the Chinese then began to set up large embassies in Africa. Their courting of anti-Western movements and disaffected dissidents like the Kenyan Oginga

Odinga reinforced these fears. In 1964, a year after Zhou's tour, the Chinese mission in Africa was beginning to veer out of control because of this failure to grasp the strength of African conservatism, buttressed by new policies in China itself. A different, more rigidly dogmatic breed of diplomats appeared on the scene in place of their pragmatic predecessors, and the era of the Chinese as missionaries gave way to the period of the Chinese as troublemakers.

The rise of the cult of Mao in China after 1964 was reflected in its relations with Africa. Although the idea of the Cultural Revolution did strike a chord in many African countries struggling against official corruption and the cultural invasion of the West (as seen for example in the Green Guards in Tanzania), the degeneration of these campaigns into scenes of anarchy and thuggery were inevitably blamed on the Chinese. Although they had no hand in the Cultural Revolution-type disturbances in Tanzania, Mali and Guinea, the dogmatism of the Chinese diplomats inevitably lost them many friends. The sending of four million 'Little Red Books' to Mali, one for every member of that tiny country's population, was cited by worried African leaders as irrefutable proof of Chinese designs on the continent. Nkrumah's fall from power in Ghana, and coups in the Central African Republic and Mali, confirmed failure in Africa. Conservative governments broke or froze relations with the Chinese People's Republic, and it was not until 1969, with the return of the experienced diplomats, that mildness returned to the relationship.

Another reason for Mao's failure in Africa was his attempt to make China's enemies Africa's 'enemies'. While promoting African independence, the Chinese also fought their own battles on African soil. Initially the link was the fight against Western imperialism, which for the Chinese was represented by the United States. As the European powers began to retreat from Africa, so the US moved into their place. The Chinese then linked their own experiences against the Americans with the rise of US intervention in both Asia and Africa, represented by Vietnam and the Congo. American paranoia about Chinese Communism, however, gradually turned more Africans towards the Chinese than the Chinese won themselves, as the extreme anti-Communist stance of the United States appeared to carry the insinuation that Africans were unable to administer their own affairs.

The second battle which the People's Republic fought on African soil was against its compatriots in Taiwan. Many African nations made a point of recognizing the People's Republic to show their independence from the US, and the growing numbers of African countries in the United Nations represented a clear threat to Taiwan's seat on the Security Council. In some cases the Beijing government supported dissident movements in the interest of gaining recognition; when Haile Selassie of Ethiopia failed to establish diplomatic relations with China following Zhou's African tour, Chinese aid was handed over to his Eritrean rebels instead.

Most African nations felt sympathy for the People's Republic, however, and saw that through their own unity they could gain entry for the Chinese Communists in the UN. In October 1971, the People's Republic finally gained the necessary two-thirds majority of votes in a motion sponsored by Mali and Swaziland. This battle between the People's Republic and its opponents on Taiwan was not as unpopular as the Sino–American arguments, for another reason. African countries held the upper hand in the establishment of diplomatic relations, and could get increased economic aid included in a recognition package.

At Bandung, Zhou had spoken about the need for Afro–Asian unity, vaulting over political differences and escaping from the sphere of the two superpowers involved in the Cold War. The Sino–Soviet split was to culminate, however, in the destruction of this myth of Chinese impartiality. African leaders were unwilling to identify with either side in the duel between the Chinese and the Russians (as they had been able to with the Sino–American duel) or exploit it for their own benefit (as they had with the People's Republic–Taiwan duel). This mystifying extraneous quarrel between Communists threatened their freedom of manoeuvre and split young Communist parties across the African continent as the Chinese began supporting splinter groups from revolutionary movements which refused to break away from the Soviet line.

Many African officials who had previously respected and

admired the Chinese for their idealistic non-interference, now became disillusioned with Chinese *realpolitik*. As one Kenyan delegate to one of the Afro-Asian synods complained:

> We are not Marxist-Leninists. Most of us have not read a line of *Das Kapital*, so what interest do you expect us to take in your doctrinal quarrels? I am tired of being asked what I think of the Soviet position when I am eating a sandwich, and what I think of the Chinese position when I am drinking my tea. I would like to be able to eat in peace.[10]

Although the returning moderate diplomats managed to paper over most of the excesses of the 'Red Guard' diplomacy of their predecessors, the altruism in the China–Africa relationship vanished. Beijing's emphasis on the threat of the USSR in Africa led the Chinese diplomats to court new friends, no matter what their political hue. One such was the US-backed president of Zaïre, Mobutu Sese Seko, whom Mao had attempted to overthrow during the early 1960s. In 1973 he was invited to Beijing and feted by Chinese leaders. 'I wasted a lot of money and arms trying to overthrow you,' Mao told him ruefully on his arrival. 'Well,' Mobutu cheerfully replied, 'you backed the wrong man.'[11]

The Chinese tried to justify their policy change by saying that it was up to the Africans to choose their own leaders, be they dictators, emperors or democratic presidents. But their involvement in Angola brought cries of incredulity from their former friends on the continent. In the 1960s the Chinese had switched their support away from the Soviet-backed MPLA to the weaker National Union for the Total Liberation of Angola (UNITA). In 1974, when Beijing was strengthening its ties with the US, the Chinese delivered a large consignment of weapons to the National Front for the Liberation of Angola (FNLA), which had its headquarters in Zaïre. In 1975 civil war broke out between the Soviet-backed MPLA and the Chinese-backed FNLA in Angola. The FNLA's light weapons were no match for the MPLA, so the Chinese once again turned their attention to UNITA.

The sight of two Communist powers fighting their battles by proxy in Angola led to a sea change in the mood of many African leaders, including Beijing's closest ally in Africa, Julius Nyerere of Tanzania. He promptly confiscated the consignment of Chinese weaponry intended for UNITA, and, following the South African invasion of Angola, the Chinese completely withdrew their support from either UNITA or the FNLA. If the Chinese had left it there, they might have come away from the situation with some credibility intact. Even after the South African invasion, however, the Chinese, apparently oblivious to deep-seated sensitivities over the apartheid issue, still refused to approve the MPLA – because it was Soviet-backed.

Post-1969 African policy was not a total disaster for China. There were Soviet-backed regimes where Chinese diplomats criticized Soviet intervention but not the indigenous rulers themselves. Then they began to turn to the West, and in particular the US, to tighten the screws on the Soviets, by invoking the bogey of the Soviet threat in Africa. Conservative African governments looked on the Chinese as friends, and the Russians, who had replaced the Chinese in backing dissident factions, as enemies. Many Africans still preferred the Chinese because of their enthusiasm, their status as the only Third World power with a permanent seat on the UN Security Council, the applicability of Maoism as an independent development model and the fact that the Soviets were European. Indeed the overthrow of the 'whatever' faction in Beijing's corridors of power, and the implementation of Deng Xiaoping's pragmatic reforms, were a great shock to some idealistic Africans, who clung to a vision of China which no longer existed.

A major reason for the continued goodwill towards China was the economic support which China had given Africa since the 1950s. In 1956 Mao had stated that 'China ought to have made a greater contribution to humanity', and with this in mind Zhou Enlai devised eight principles for Chinese economic aid to Africa. Compared with the stringent demands made by Western donors, and given that China was itself a Third World country struggling to develop, Zhou's eight principles were seen as praiseworthy proof of Chinese idealism. Loans came with no political demands, were often free of interest and with long-term repayment beginning only after the project was completed. Chinese experts lived in the same conditions as their African hosts, and were thus the standard bearers of Mao's philanthropic crusade to Africa.

Compared with Western loans, the amount of money donated by China between 1960 and 1980 was relatively small, but many of the projects which were undertaken underlined Chinese dedication to African development. The centrepiece was the Tanzam railway. Landlocked Zambia was dependent on South Africa and Rhodesia for its trade routes during the 1950s and 1960s, and was thus in a geopolitical stranglehold. One possible route for Zambian trade was via Tanzania to the Indian Ocean, but Western banks, including the World Bank, were unwilling to provide the necessary funds to construct a railway line, because it was considered economically unviable.

In 1970 China offered a financial and technical support package which included the loan of $400 million and 25,000 Chinese technicians, the building of 300 bridges, six miles of tunnel and ninety-three stations, and the supply of eighty-five locomotives, 2,100 freight wagons and 100 passenger coaches. In 1974, this Tanzam railway, the longest railway built anywhere since the Second World War, was completed, two years ahead of schedule. For the Chinese, however, their problems were only just beginning.

Part of the agreement between China and Zambia and Tanzania had been that while Chinese technicians were building the railway, they would educate and train enough local personnel to take their place once the task had been completed. The Chinese technicians, however, were not at ease teaching across such a wide cultural gulf and saw themselves as working not primarily for the Africans themselves, but as volunteers for China. Although Mao had used the example of the Canadian doctor Norman Bethune, who had served in the Red Army during the civil war, as one of his three major planks for promoting internationalism during the Cultural Revolution, he and Zhou had to sell the costly Chinese economic aid programme to party critics as a heroic crusade for Chinese people to become involved in.

In many places, Chinese technicians did better than their

European counterparts, particularly in the health sector, where Chinese doctors went further into the rural areas and shared a similar background in the use of herbal medicine. Other Chinese technicians sought to counter European paternalism towards Africa by a show of brotherly respect. Where this did not succeed, however, the result was a serious blow to Chinese pride. The Chinese were good at building railways but not good at crossing cultural frontiers to teach others to do so. In 1976 the Tanzam railway virtually ground to a halt, because of the failure of the Chinese training programme and the withdrawal of the Chinese specialists back to China. In a move which was duplicated across the African continent, the Chinese had to be asked to return and sort out the problems.

The Chinese, who had invested so many resources, both human and financial, into these projects, were thus humiliated. In China itself, some officials were in any case questioning whether China could afford to send so many skilled technicians abroad when the domestic economy desperately cried out for skilled workers. After Deng's rise to power in 1978 China began concentrating on its own development problems, and the donation of free aid and maintenance declined rapidly.

China's newest African policy was summed up by Hu Yaobang, then Secretary General of the Communist Party, in 1984:

> To those poor countries that are facing difficult times and are being invaded and threatened, if possible, we will give military and economic support and assistance. On military assistance, the Central Committee has a general rule to charge only for basic expenses. For economic assistance, the experience of history has shown that the method of giving completely gratis benefits neither side.[12]

Although China was close to the US in the 1980s, Deng shied away from being drawn into Cold War hostilities against the Soviets, and in courting a body of sympathetic supporting countries in world diplomacy, Chinese eyes were once again drawn towards Africa. In 1982 Premier Zhao Ziyang followed the route which Zhou Enlai had taken almost twenty years earlier through Africa – but with one important new component – that of using Africa as a market for Chinese goods, cheaper than Western goods, and available in greater volume. The profits could fund aid projects, or be reinvested with African companies into joint ventures benefiting both sides. Tazara, the company formed to oversee the day-to-day running of the Tanzam railway, showed its first working profit in 1984.

As the 1980s progressed, the Chinese began voicing more anti-American rhetoric and reverted to their former role of aiding guerrilla movements fighting against the remnants of imperialism in Africa. Sam Nujoma, the SWAPO leader, and Oliver Tambo, President of the ANC, both paid visits to Beijing. The Chinese premise remained unchanged, that China and Africa faced identical problems and should support each other, but now the Chinese leadership preferred to emphasize the economic fellowship between the two partners. By supporting Salim Salim of Tanzania in his attempt to become Secretary General of the UN, the Chinese clearly positioned themselves with the underdeveloped South in its duel with the economically dominant North.

The failure of the training programmes in Africa had led to more African students being educated in China. But this only served to publicize how deep-seated the racist feelings were among the Chinese general public. Traditionally, the Chinese viewed black people as stupid and uncivilized, and Kang Youwei, the Chinese reformer at the turn of the century, had even recommended the forced deportation of Africans to Canada, whose sunless climate would change their black pigmentation and 'allow' them eventually to join the golden (Chinese) and silver (European) races. The Chinese leaders tried to point up the similarities between the two cultures – the peasant base of society, filial loyalty and the importance of close personal ties. Finally, Chinese technicians were sent back to Africa to learn from the Africans, and to work with them on their common development problems.

Philip Snow wrote, in his account of China's relations with Africa, *The Star Raft,*

Sometimes, to begin with, the Chinese leaders failed to understand certain African sensibilities. But they went home, assessed their mistakes and returned with new policies better attuned to the continent's aspirations and needs. As a result of their efforts China has often been more successful, in its collective political and economic dealings with Africa, than the various European adversaries with which it has vied.[13]

In Asia the impact of the Chinese Communist victory was immense, in all sectors of society. For the working people it demonstrated the potential of peasants' or workers' parties, masterminded by a Marxist leadership. For Asian intellectuals, it represented a direct challenge to the Gandhian-Nehruvian model of non-violent political independence, while raising traditional fears of Chinese domination of the Asian political scene. Even Asian businessmen welcomed the change in the Chinese government, offering them potential access to a stable unified market of hundreds of millions of people, regulated by officials who would not, it was claimed, be adding 'sweeteners' to the cost of business deals.

Zhou Enlai argued in 1951,

Under the influence of the Chinese revolution, the level of consciousness of the Asian people has been raised to an unprecedented degree, and liberation movements are developing more and more strongly with each passing day. The unity of the Chinese people and the peoples of Asia will certainly create a powerful and matchless force in the Far East which will rapidly push forward the great wheel of history in the movement for the independence and liberation of the peoples of Asian countries.[14]

During the Korean War, the Chinese stressed the need to help rebel movements across the Asian continent against their 'bourgeois' nationalist rulers, following Mao's dictum that it was 'impossible for a genuine people's revolution to win victory in any country without various forms of help from the international revolutionary forces'.[15] After the Bandung Conference, with the rise of the policy of revolution through a 'united front from above', Beijing began cultivating ties with nationalist Asian governments, while assuring Asian leaders that China did not intend to subvert its neighbours. Whilst China continued to be admired by many Asian workers and intellectuals, however, the rise of a distinctive Maoist foreign policy, which sought to challenge the contradictions inherent in the 'united front from above' policy, inevitably led China to act in a more antagonistic manner.

The first arena for such contradictions concerned China's borders. On coming to power, the attitude of the Chinese Communist leaders towards their Asian neighbours was a mixture of intense national pride in their own achievements and intellectual shame over the expansionist policies of their imperial predecessors. Mao, as we have already noted, had highlighted the effects of Western imperialism on China's former vassal states, and had thus linked the Chinese struggle with the independence movements in Indonesia, India, and the countries of South East Asia. However, when these statements were set alongside one of his remarks to Edgar Snow in 1936, that, 'It is the immediate task of China to regain all our lost territories', many Asian leaders were understandably nervous.

For the first five years of the People's Republic, many Indians were seduced by the chanting of *Hindi Chini bhai bhai* ('Indians and Chinese are brothers'), and during the Korean War the Indian Ambassador in Beijing, K.M. Pannikar, became a crucial go-between for Chinese foreign relations with the West. In 1954 Nehru visited Beijing, where he and Zhou Enlai announced their adherence to the Panch Shila. The frontier between the two countries remained unclarified, however, as the Chinese attempted to locate missing documents and the Indians appeared satisfied with the status quo.

Relations between the two countries then deteriorated because of Mao's growing distrust of Nehru and the Indian shock over Chinese repression in Tibet in 1959. Minor border skirmishes began to occur. The frontier was based in one sector on the so-called McMahon Line, which had been established in a treaty signed between the British and the Chinese Imperial Court. If the Chinese accepted the McMahon Line, then they could be expected to accept the other unequal treaties which the Imperial Court had signed during the previous century – and which had inspired Mao and his colleagues to revolt in the first place.

The Sino–Indian border war, triggered by a swift attack by the Chinese in 1962, can thus be seen as an attempt by the Chinese to humiliate an Indian government apparently clinging to the laws laid down by their former imperialist masters, and thus ridicule the independence that Nehru had achieved. Simultaneously, it was a warning to India not to interfere in China's internal affairs in Tibet. The Chinese then began offering their support to the Naga minority group in India, just as they did for minority groups in Thailand and Burma when those two countries became critical of China's border policy.

A similar pattern can be detected in the Sino–Vietnam War of 1979. Divergent Sino–Vietnamese blueprints for Indo-China, and mistreatment of ethnic Chinese resident in Vietnam, were important factors in China's decision to invade Vietnam. When the Vietnamese began arguing that their common border with China should be realigned according to the treaties drawn up between the French and the Imperial Chinese Court, China was ideologically straitjacketed. For over thirty years China had been supporting the Vietnamese in their struggle against French and American imperialism, and now the Vietnamese had the audacity to demand a border settlement on the old French terms. The invasion was officially explained as a 'counter-attack in self-defence', but Deng Xiaoping gave a clear indication of the Chinese mentality behind these border disputes when he remarked that the invasion was launched to 'teach Vietnam a lesson'.[16]

On the border issues, the *realpolitik* behind China's pro-nouncements of Asianness soon became clear – although it did not intend to re-create its former imperial vassal states by force, it would 'never allow any other country to tamper with its territory'.[17] Gradually, then, the thin veneer covering China's ideological stance of peaceful co-existence began to crack and the peoples of Asia realized that China would still maintain its national interests ahead of any ideological stance of united Asianness.

China's relations with other Asian Communist parties followed a similar descent from grandiose schemes of independent Asian revolution to earthier concerns of national interest. In November 1949 Mao sent a message to the Secretary General of the Indian Communist Party, making no attempt to hide his belief that India had not yet completed its revolution. 'I firmly believe that India, relying on the brave Communist Party of India and the unity and struggle of all Indian patriots, will certainly not remain long under the yoke of imperialism and its collaborators.'[18] (This was two years after Nehru had taken office as Prime Minister of an independent India.)

During the 1950s the chief threat to the Chinese in Asia had come from the Americans, and Beijing's foreign policy therefore sought to highlight the spectre of Western imperialism. By underlining their own Asianness, the Chinese hoped to deny the Americans access to the region. They provided political backing for anti-American groups in the Philippines and Japan. In Thailand, Beijing began sponsoring a 'people's war' in the north east. China supported leftist groups in Malaysia and Singapore, and backed Indonesia's attempt to crush the Malaysian Federation, regarding the Malaysian government as an extension of British colonialism.

Chinese influence in the Indian Communist Party rested mainly on rural supporters, but when the Tibetan uprising and the Sino–Indian War were followed by the wooing of the Indians by the Soviets, Chinese ideological credibility declined drastically. In Singapore, the Communist Party presented only a limited challenge to the rigidly anti-Communist Lee Kuan Yew. After 1956, therefore, Mao turned his attentions to President Sukarno of Indonesia, whom he saw as the best available partner in Asia (and the Third World) against growing Soviet leverage and continuing Western influence. In D.N. Aidit he also found a Marxist theoretician who shared his own views on the importance of the peasantry in the revolutionary struggle. But aligning China so closely to the Indonesian Party was a tactical error of some magnitude. Following the 1965 attempted coup, which the new military regime of Suharto blamed on China, Mao lost all possible influence in Indonesia for the next twenty-five years and also set back the advancement of the Indonesian ethnic Chinese.

Most Asian Communist parties were wary of Chinese domination because of the importance of nationalism within their own policy packages and the ease with which ruling governments could dismiss them as pro-Chinese stooges. The Indonesian affair confirmed such an analysis. China's support for Pakistan in its war with India in 1965 only served to lose it more friends. Russia's negotiation of the Tashkent Agreement which ended the war undermined China's arguments and increased respect for the Soviets. The final nail in the coffin was the Algerian affair. After consistently supporting the Algerian National Liberation Front in its fight for independence, the Chinese set great store by a proposed second Bandung-type Afro-Asian conference in Algiers in 1965. Here, it was hoped, the Chinese would be able to gather Communist parties from all over the Third World behind them in their doctrinal quarrel with the USSR. But the host President, Ben Bella, was overthrown in a coup in June, just before the planned conference, and the Chinese quickly recognized the new right-wing government in order to facilitate the holding of the conference on schedule. The message the Chinese thus gave to their allies was one of indifference to principle.

By 1972, with President Nixon's visit to China, all hopes that Beijing would put principles before its own national interests had foundered. In 1963 Mao had told a group of African visitors that 'our unity is not one of race: it is the unity of comrades and friends'.[19] But if the memoirs of Alexander Haig, who went to Beijing in 1972, are to be believed, it is clear that China then saw itself solely as a big power player. 'I reported to President Nixon,' Haig wrote, 'that the impact of what [Zhou] said to me was: don't lose in Vietnam; don't withdraw from South East Asia.'[20]

While continually maintaining their belief in the need for Asian revolutions to originate in their own countries, and thereby follow the Chinese example, Mao's statements reveal a traditional Chinese disdain for Asian comrades. When the anti-Communist Thai Premier Kukrit Pramoj asked Mao in 1975 how to crush the Thai Communist Party, Mao replied: 'You don't have to worry about the Communist Party of Thailand. It has existed for more than ten years but not a single Thai Communist has come to see me here.'[21]

One Thai ex-Communist, however, interviewed in 1975, explained that, 'The Thought of Mao is modern Marxism-Leninism. It is the only thing that can change the world. Only those who hold to the Thought of Mao can destroy obstacles.'[22] Chiranand Pitpreecha, a leader of the 1973 student uprising in Thailand, joined the Thai Communist guerrillas, but quickly became disillusioned with the influence of the Chinese Party. 'Many of the old cadres were of Chinese origin and could not even speak Thai properly. We were annoyed because we were concerned with our own revolution. We didn't care whether Jiang Qing or Zhou Enlai were fighting each other or not in Beijing.'[23]

Mao could not see that very few of the new Asian leaders were willing to 'struggle against imperialism', because of the risks of armed combat with the West, just as he viewed the problems of the Third World solely through the prism of his own revolutionary career. China's own experience in dealing with the social and economic problems of development should have increased its prestige in the Third World. However, it was unable to exploit this, and Mao's belief in 'politics in command' only served to alienate those people who had looked to the Chinese victory in 1949 as an example from which the Third World could learn. Domestic policies were too fast-changing, and too embroiled in secret intra-Party factionalism, to be suitable fodder for foreign followers.

The elimination of the 'whatever clique' and the elevation of 'economics in command' in the late 1970s and the 1980s helped to recover some of China's lost ground in both Africa and Asia. China's relations with Hong Kong have actually followed a consistent policy of 'economics in command' since 1949, apart from a hiccup during the Cultural Revolution when local hotheads seriously undermined the prestige of the Chinese Communist Party in the territory. Deng's remark in the late 1980s that he would endorse a Chief Executive of Hong Kong after 1997 even if he was a triad leader, as long as he were a patriot, illustrates Chinese thinking.[24] The open-door policy which Deng has implemented has necessarily brought China into contact with former enemies in South Korea, Japan and even Taiwan. China's foreign policy in Asia is currently, as Michael Yahuda has written, 'issue-orientated rather than centred on opposition to a principal enemy'.[25]

The Tiananmen Square massacre of June 1989 did not seriously threaten this process of rapprochement. China announced afterwards that it would take 'unity and co-operation with Third World countries, including African countries, as the fundamental foothold of its foreign policy', and the first visitors to Beijing following the Tiananmen massacre were indeed from Africa.[26] Realistically, however, this would appear to mean the continued use of Africa as a market, and it has been followed by steps into Latin America (where historically the impact of Chinese Communism has been negated by Cuban dependence on Soviet aid) and the Middle East. Although the Shining Path in Peru continues to preach Maoist doctrines, the Chinese leaders profess indifference to it. Indeed, as well as new Sino–Cuban economic pledges and the exchange of official delegations, the main thrust of China's recent diplomatic drive in Latin America has been towards that region's capitalist countries.

Diplomatic relations with Indonesia were reopened at last in 1990, enabling the Chinese to treat the ASEAN countries on a collective regional basis. The crumbling of Communism in Eastern Europe and the USSR during 1989 and 1990 led to an improvement in Sino–Vietnamese relations, although the problem of Cambodia continued to be a fly in the ointment. 'When you analyse Vietnamese and Chinese traditions,' a Vietnamese official admitted in 1990, 'you see some accidental similarities, but it's clear we have different approaches to a lot of problems.'[27]

That diagnosis would fit most of China's relationships with Third World countries over the past forty years. The failure of the Chinese Communists was their inability to learn from their own experiences and change their policies accordingly. China, it seemed, was too engrossed with its frequent turnabouts in policy – from the co-operatives to the communes, from back-yard steel furnaces to industrial de-control, from 'walking on two legs' to the open door – to be able to indoctrinate foreign acolytes in their breathless transitions. More importantly, the contradictions within Chinese Communist foreign policy resulted in more attention being paid to the struggle against imperialism and social-imperialism. The idealism of the 1950s was quickly replaced by *realpolitik*. As Hu Yaobang put it more tactfully, in a talk to Italian Communists in 1986: 'The facts prove that there is no one pat formula, that the textbooks give us no ready-made set of replies to the question of how different countries should move toward or build socialism. Ultimately, socialism still emerges from practice.'[28]

6 *Marxism vs. Nationalism* –
The Question of the Superpowers:
I. USSR

At the Second Comintern Congress in July 1920, a year before the Chinese Communist Party was founded, two extreme views were advanced as to the correct path for the international revolutionary movement to follow. Serratti of Italy put forward the 'Occidental' line, which minimalized the position of Asia at the very time that the prospects of European revolution were dwindling. M.N. Roy of India countered with an 'Oriental' line, arguing that revolution in the colonies was a *sine qua non* of proletarian revolution in Europe. Lenin was willing to equate the importance of Asia and Europe, but opposed the elevation of Asia to a superior role. Instead, he identified the character of future Asian revolutions as nationalist, and proposed the formation of united fronts with other nationalist movements.

In his *Left-Wing Communism – An Infantile Disorder*, Lenin stated:

> As long as national and state differences exist among peoples and countries – and these differences will continue to exist for a very long time even after the dictatorship of the proletariat has been established on a world scale – the unity of international tactics of the communist working class movement of all countries demands, not the elimination of variety, not the abolition of national differences (that is a foolish dream at the present), but such an application of the fundamental principles of communism (soviet power and the dictatorship of the proletariat) as will correctly modify these principles in certain particulars, correctly adapt and apply them to national and national-state differences.[1]

The ascendancy of the Soviet Communist Party in influencing

the growth and development of Chinese Communism has been manifold. In the 1920s the nascent Soviet government had more sway over Chinese politics than the Western powers did. After the West refused help to Sun Yat-sen, Comintern advisers assisted him in reorganizing the political structure of the Guomindang along Soviet lines, and creating a united front within which the 423 members of the Communist Party could work. In 1922, Mao declared the organization of the Chinese people into this democratic united front as part of the world revolution against imperialism. From the very beginning of their movement, the Chinese Communists were able to give equal weight to both their revolutionary and their nationalist credentials.

The rise of Jiang Jieshi and the right wing of the Guomindang Party after Sun's death in 1924 did not alter the Comintern directives. The merits of the 'united front from above' policy went on being argued, even when Jiang made his bid for power over the left-wing Nationalist, Wang Jingwei, in Guangzhou in 1926. In February 1927, Jiang publicly announced his intention of eliminating Communists from the ranks of the Guomindang. The Central Executive Committee of the Party, which was broadly left-wing, responded by reducing Jiang's rank to army commander and taking away his seat in the government. Jiang's massacre of the Communists in Shanghai and other southern cities proved, however, that he held the reins of power within the Nationalist movement, and he established his own government in Nanjing.

The Russian Bolshevik Party had undergone a similar period of struggle since the death of Lenin: by 1927 Stalin had only just beaten off the challenge of Trotsky to become the undisputed head of the Soviet (and thereby world) revolutionary movement. At the end of 1926 he continued to urge his Chinese 'comrades' to work within the united front alliance, developing relations with the left wing of the Guomindang. His telegram to M.N. Roy immediately after the Shanghai massacre, urging the arming of 20,000 Communist Party members and 50,000 workers and peasants, did nothing to placate fears of Russian imperialism on the part of the left wing of the Guomindang.[2] On 15 July 1927, the Wuhan-based government of the Guomindang expelled the Communist Party from its midst. Stalin's insistence on the maintenance of the united front to further the national, rather than the social revolution, would long be remembered by the Chinese Communists.

Following the events of 1927, the Chinese Communists were forced to take the revolution underground in the urban areas, while Mao and Zhu De concentrated on the peasant struggle. Lenin had stated that, 'We are, in a sense, pupils of the peasants',[3] and in 1926 Stalin reaffirmed Lenin's policy in a directive to the Comintern. 'The most important task of the Chinese Communist Party is to win the peasant masses for active struggle on behalf of fighting slogans which link political and economic demands comprehensible to and important to the peasantry.'[4] But Stalin in 1927 forbade the formation of peasant 'soviets' until the next revolutionary upsurge in China, whereas Mao called for the immediate formation of Communist bases. Relations between the two parties began to reveal signs of the leadership struggle that eventually led to the split in the 1960s.

When the putschist policies of Li Lisan collapsed, Wang Ming, one of the '28 Returned Students' who had been educated in the USSR and was closely linked with Stalin, took over the leadership mantle. The removal of the Central Committee from Shanghai to Mao's Jiangxi 'soviet' during the early 1930s enhanced the threat to the Moscow-imposed line of Mao's theories of revolutionary struggle and began to realign the '28 Students' behind an indigenous Chinese form of Marxism. Before the First Front Red Army was forced out of its Jiangxi base by Jiang Jieshi, to undertake its Long March to northern China, policy directives continued to bear the imprint of Moscow, through the guiding hand of the Comintern representative Otto Braun. The loss of the Jiangxi base thus became another entry in the inventory of Russian failures in China.

The importance of the Zunyi conference for Sino–Soviet relations did not merely hang on Mao's breakthrough into the highest leadership echelon of the Party. His attacks on the 'military troika' of Wang Ming, Zhou Enlai and Otto Braun for their blunders in Jiangxi succeeded only through the intercession of two of the Moscow-educated comrades, Wang Jiaxiang and Luo Fu. Otto Braun was not even called to speak during the conference, despite carrying the full weight of the Soviet Party behind him. The final conference resolution, which attacked the erroneous policies of the Party when it had been under Comintern control, was carried to Moscow by Chen Yun, demonstrating the new independence of the Chinese Party. When the resolution was belatedly released in China in 1942 following Mao's Rectification Campaign, the names of two of the accused (Wang Ming and Zhou Enlai) were edited out in the name of Party unity – and also to point the finger of accusation where Mao, and, it must be added, most of his colleagues, felt it was really deserved, at the Soviet-dominated Comintern itself, through the naming of its representative, Otto Braun.

The Chinese leaders had no radio or other contact with the Comintern during the Long March, so that Braun commanded very little credibility or authority. By 1936, when the Chinese Communists arrived in Shaanxi province in the north of China, Mao had withstood another challenge for the Party leadership from Zhang Guotao, whose subsequent defection to the Guomindang further weakened the possibility of Stalin's imposing a 'unity' figurehead over two warring Communist factions. But then the 'united front from below' policy, which the Chinese had been following since 1930, was replaced by a 'united front from above' policy. This was because Japanese infiltration into China had become a national issue; by identifying themselves with the anti-Japanese struggle, the Communists were able to play the nationalism card against their Guomindang allies. When officers of the young Marshal Zhang Xueliang, the Manchurian warlord, took Jiang Jieshi prisoner, the Guomindang were compelled, as the price of his release, to establish a joint United Front against the Japanese. That gave the Communists time to regroup their forces. This policy coincided with the United Front policy of the Comintern, which would find its most infamous expression in the non-aggression pact between Stalin and Hitler in 1939.

In 1936, in an interview with the American journalist Edgar Snow, Mao said, 'We are certainly not fighting for an emancipated China in order to turn the country over to Moscow.'[5] The fundamental differences between the Russian Revolution in 1917 and the path of the Chinese revolution can be traced to social and national issues and, importantly in terms of later theoretical developments, to the locus of revolution, which in 1917 had filtered from Petrograd to the rest of the country, but in China had spread from the countryside to the cities. These two factors, the Chinese Communists' deeper and sourer experience of foreign imperialism and the differing interpretation of Marxist theory, are crucial to the understanding of the relationship between the Soviet and Chinese Communist parties. Throughout the civil war period, the Chinese played down their relations with the Soviet Party. Some Westerners therefore labelled them as a revolutionary peasant party – or as 'agrarian reformers', in John Service's famous phrase. Mao's Sinification of Marxism helped him to consolidate his position within the Party itself, but also helped to gain the full support of the Chinese people against the Guomindang, whom the Communists could easily label as American puppets.

This bid for theoretical independence matched the physical relationship between the USSR and the Chinese Communists during the Yan'an era. The battles with Germany on the Eastern European front swallowed up most of the available Soviet war materiel, and left the USSR with a deep psychological fear of a new world war which would become one of the breaking points in the Communist relationship after 1949. The Chinese had to find their own weapons, which they obtained mainly from the Americans (via the Guomindang), and the Japanese, and from armaments factories in Yan'an. Stalin was unable to turn his full attention to China until the end of the war in Europe, and his incursion into the war against Japan then had important repercussions for Sino–Soviet relations.

Throughout the Sino–Japanese War, the Russians had continued to patronize Jiang Jieshi's Guomindang, in the international political arena as well as through limited military aid. At the Yalta Conference in February 1945, Stalin had been given Western promises of a status quo in Mongolia, the whole of Sakhalin, the Kurile Islands, and Russian rights to the ports of Dairen and Port Arthur and the Chinese Zhongchun railway in return for his declaration of war against Japan – which came two days after the first American atomic bomb fell on Hiroshima. On 14 August Stalin concluded an accord with the Guomindang in which Jiang Jieshi agreed to recognize the independence of Outer Mongolia, the establishment of a joint Sino–Russian base at Port Arthur and of a free port in Dairen, and a thirty-year concession for the joint exploitation of the Zhongchun railway in Manchuria. In return, the Soviet Union promised to support the Nationalist government, refrain from intervention in China's internal affairs, and respect Chinese sovereignty in Manchuria.

Before this treaty had even been signed, Russian troops moved into Manchuria (China's burgeoning industrial heartland) in force, and as they began to fall back again when Japan surrendered, they carried away most of the industrial equipment superstructure which the Japanese had set up in the area. To the Chinese Communists, the Russians thus appeared little different from their Tsarist predecessors. In 1945, according to Vladimer Dedijer, Stalin met with Chinese Communist representatives and 'told them bluntly that we considered the development of the uprising in China had no prospects, that the Chinese comrades should seek a *modus vivendi* with Jiang Jieshi, and that they should join the Jiang Jieshi government and dissolve their army'.[6]

For the next four years, as the civil war raged in China, the Chinese Communists were isolated from Soviet aid, as Stalin continued to insist that they should come to terms with Jiang Jieshi and work within the Nationalist government. Even in 1948, when the Chinese Party's prospects of victory had soared, Stalin advised his Chinese comrades to stop at the Yangzi river and accept a divided nation. During the final year of the war, the Soviets continued to negotiate with the Guomindang government for Sino–Soviet co-operation, and the Russian Ambassador and his staff were the only foreign diplomats who followed the Nationalist government down to Guangzhou after the fall of Nanjing. Throughout May 1949, with Beijing securely held by the Chinese Communist Party, the Soviets calmly went on negotiating with the Guomindang over commercial rights in Xinjiang province.

There were reasons why Stalin did not relish the prospect of Communist success in China. First, the Chinese were winning by their own efforts, without the aid of their Soviet comrades. Second, they had in Mao Zedong a theoretician who had mapped out a path to revolutionary success different from Stalin's interpretations of Marxism, and much more successful than the Comintern-inspired programme of the 1920s. Third, the imminence of a unified China, whether Marxist or capitalist, was not something which appealed to Russians. It would threaten not only traditional Soviet border concerns, which had been highlighted by the Second World War, but also the USSR's position as leader of the world revolutionary movement. According to John Paton Davies, a United States diplomat in China in 1949, the Chinese Communists would 'be able to throw their weight around in South East Asia more effectively than Moscow can. The spectre of a great autocephalous competitor may well have disturbed the Kremlin's dreams.'[7]

In his *On New Democracy*, Mao had stated that 'as the struggle between the Socialist country and the Imperialist countries is becoming sharper and sharper, it becomes absolutely necessary that China makes her choice between two camps'.[8] By 1949 that choice had apparently been made. In *On the People's Democratic Dictatorship*, Mao said that China would 'externally, unite in a common struggle with those nations of the world which treat us as equals and unite with the peoples of all countries. That is, ally ourselves with the Soviet Union, with the People's Democracies and with the proletariat and the broad masses of the people in all other countries, and form an international united front.'[9] This apparent forgive-and-forget attitude of the Chinese Communists, however, did not mean that they were willing to become puppets of Soviet masters.

The formative years of the Chinese revolution were a direct response to foreign incursions into China, and the Chinese Party's acceptance of Lenin's theory of imperialism meant that it took the Soviet Union as the natural leader of the socialist bloc, whatever mistakes may have been made during the course of the Chinese revolution. There is some evidence that Mao was driven by Stalin into publicly declaring his allegiance to Moscow. According to a US State Department report, the Soviet leaders were unhappy with the popularity of *On New Democracy* in some East European satellite countries and had sent an emissary to brief the new Chinese leaders in Beijing. 'Mao [was] indignant and helpless in [the] face

[of] powerful Soviet forces along [the] border', the report stated.[10]

The dire condition of the Chinese economy also obliged the Chinese leaders either to adopt a totally self-reliant economic policy or to look elsewhere for foreign aid. Mao's *On the People's Democratic Dictatorship* had already dismissed Western bankers and financiers as possible sources of aid, and the economic blockade of Shanghai by the Guomindang in 1949, coupled with the devastation of Manchurian industry after Soviet pilfering and four years of civil war, forced the Chinese to turn to the Russians. On 1 August 1949, a one-year trade pact was signed between the USSR and the North East administration in China, followed on 14 February 1950 by the Sino–Soviet Treaty of Friendship, Alliance and Mutual Assistance.

On the surface, the Treaty confirmed Cold War suspicions about the 'loss' of China to the Communist bloc. It was primarily aimed against the Japanese, with the idea of preventing any 'repetition of aggression and violation of peace on the part of Japan or any other state which should unite in any form with Japan in acts of aggression'.[11] This was a clear warning to the USA, whose influence in Japan was of concern to both the Chinese and Soviet Communists, without referring to the American role in the Chinese civil war. The treaty also contained a provision for consultation on 'all important international problems affecting the common interests of the Soviet Union and China', without giving any specific material indications of Soviet support for their Chinese comrades.[12]

The friction which had spoilt the relationship between the two Communist parties before 1949 had not disappeared. Mao left Beijing unannounced, amid high local security, apparently pressurized to leave his country for the very first time and go to Moscow, on the pretence of celebrating the seventieth birthday of Stalin. Travelling by train, Mao arrived in Moscow on 16 December, and soon made it clear that he would not tolerate being treated like an East European satellite leader. As Chen Boda, his ideological mouthpiece, had noted in a special article just beforehand, the People's Republic of China, unlike the East European countries, was 'founded on the pattern of the Bolshevism of Lenin and Stalin without the traditions of Social Democracy'.[13] Although Liu Shaoqi and Gao Gang, both members of the Central Committee, had been to Moscow for preliminary talks to set the stage for Mao's visit, and N.V. Roschin, the Soviet Ambassador, had come to Beijing with the draft agreement, it soon became apparent that the talks were not going well.

After arriving at Moscow station, and delaying his disembarkation because, according to one witness, he was afraid of assassination, Mao had a brief meeting in the Kremlin. Here Stalin, backed by Beria, Malenkov, Bulganin, Kaganovitch and Vishinski, welcomed Mao: 'You are so young. So healthy.' Mao replied, 'I have been attacked and pushed aside for a long time', thereby alluding to the Soviets' attitude to the Chinese since 1921. After more exchanges, Stalin asked Mao, 'Now that you have finally arrived, tell us: what shall we do?' Mao's reply totally confused the Soviet old guard. 'We must make something which is both good-looking and tasty,' he declared mysteriously.[14] The Russians were perplexed, and cancelled the talks planned for the next two days. Having made the Russians realize that he wanted concrete action over the Sino–Soviet Treaty which Stalin had signed with Jiang Jieshi, Mao sent for Zhou Enlai to negotiate a new treaty.

The Chinese continued to play cat and mouse with their Russian comrades, as Zhou also travelled by train, stopping at practically every station along the route to Moscow to promote the new bonds between the two giant countries. But Stalin was not impressed. Control of Manchuria was crucial to him. The Zhongchun railway provided the Russians with a short cut to their vital warm-water military port of Vladivostok, and consequently stirred passions like those aroused in Anglo-Saxon breasts by the Suez and Panama canals. Apart from the official agreement and the secret settlements, the Chinese were made to swallow some very unsavoury proposals. They were never to raise again the issue of Outer Mongolian independence (which meant its *de facto* dependence on the USSR rather than on China); all Soviet citizens in China, who on paper were technical advisers but were in practice agents of the Kremlin trying to manipulate the Chinese Party from within, would enjoy extra-territorial jurisdiction; Soviet advisers were not to be pulled out of Port Dairen until 1954; and control over the Zhongchun railway was not to be returned to the Chinese until 1958.

In his famous de-Stalinization speech of 1956, Khrushchev commented on this Sino–Soviet Treaty, alleging that 'Stalin faced Mao Zedong with a series of economic demands smacking of colonialism. He insisted that he, Stalin, must have the final word on the development of Communism within China as he had in other countries of the Soviet bloc.'[15] In the same year, Mao stated that getting Stalin to commit himself to making economic concessions to China and giving financial aid had been like taking 'meat from a tiger's mouth'.[16] The concessions which the Chinese won were paltry. In the third agreement under the treaty, the Soviet Union was to lend the Chinese $300 million, to be repaid in rare and non-ferrous metals well below their international market value. Mao had asked for more than ten times that amount, and on returning to Beijing, he found that the rouble had been devalued by 20 per cent, slashing the final value of the agreement by $60 million. By comparison the US gave the Guomindang more than $2,000 million between August 1945 and 1949.[17]

Mao showed his dissatisfaction by failing even to mention the aid figure in his speech to the Central Committee on 6 June 1950. His refusal to be fobbed off by the Russians increased his popularity in China, but now the Chinese had to implement a treaty which bore many resemblances to that between the Guomindang government and the USSR. Sino–Soviet Friendship associations were nevertheless established throughout the country; Soviet writings were translated on every subject; the First Five Year Plan was directly modelled on Lenin's first economic plan; and Russian was made the official first foreign language.

The strain continued, however, as Stalin went on meddling in China's internal affairs, trying to control the development of Communism in China. The first area of contention was Xinjiang province in north-west China, which had a history of Soviet infiltration. In 1944, the Turki population in the Ili region of Xinjiang had revolted against the Guomindang and with Russian help had set up a 'Republic of East Turkestan'. By 1947 there were reports that the whole of North Xinjiang was economically detached from China. In September 1949, however, General Zhang Zhizhong, the former Guomindang representative in Xinjiang, and Saifudin, an important leader of the Turki movement, went to Beijing to take part in the People's Consultative Conference, and the Xinjiang government declared its allegiance to the People's Republic.

Before he left for Moscow, Mao had invited Xinjiang government leaders to Beijing for further talks to boost their commitment to China and re-emphasize the Party's support for them. The aeroplane carrying them back to Xinjiang mysteriously crashed, however, killing all aboard and leaving Soviet influence over the province unabated. This helps to explain Mao's caution about his mode of transport to Moscow. The Treaty which he signed there contained a clause which indicated Stalin's refusal to relinquish his hold on Xinjiang. While recognizing Beijing's *de facto* control over the province, the treaty stated that joint stock companies would be established for the exploitation of oil and mineral resources under the 'direction' of Soviet experts, a stratagem which Stalin had used to great effect in placating Eastern European demands for more independence from Moscow.

Stalin similarly refused to allow the Chinese direct control over Manchuria. In September 1949, before the establishment of the People's Republic, General Malinovski, the Soviet military commander in Manchuria in 1945–6, had brought a military mission to Harbin as a show of strength and to follow up the trade pact between the North East Administration and the Soviet Union a month earlier. These actions served only to antagonize the Chinese, as they appeared hardly more moral than the unequal treaties of the imperialist powers. The Soviets failed to keep their promises to return industrial machinery, and material assistance was sold at inflated prices.[18] Even worse, secret advisers gradually gained control of the most important industries, for example, the soyabean industry which had a potential annual export value of £60 million. The population in Manchuria was unanimously anti-Soviet because of the patronizing attitudes of the Russian comrades.[19] The two trade pacts had involved the forced export of foodstuffs from China via Manchuria to the USSR, at a time when there was an internal grain shortage and prices were particularly vulnerable.

It was not only in the economic arena that Stalin applied pressure to the new Chinese leaders. In November 1948, Angus Ward, the US Consul General, had been placed under house arrest on suspicion of spying by the Chinese authorities in Shenyang. This incident helped to sour Sino–American relations during 1949, providing ammunition for the China Lobby in the US for the non-recognition of the People's Republic. There is some evidence that Soviet infiltration, and a pro-Soviet faction within the Chinese Party, were responsible for the Ward case, with the intention of increasing Mao's dependence on Moscow.[20]

When the Russians made Mao travel to Moscow and conclude the treaty almost as soon as he came to power, they knew (through their spy in the British Foreign Office, Guy Burgess) that the Americans and British were still considering recognizing Communist China. When Jacob Malik, the Russian Ambassador at the United Nations, walked out of the Security Council in protest against the continued presence of the Chinese Guomindang delegate, he did so in the knowledge that he would leave the Chinese Communists internationally isolated and totally dependent on the USSR for economic and political goodwill. The culmination of this process came in June 1950, with the North Korean invasion of South Korea.

In 1949, Kim Il Sung, the North Korean Moscow-trained Communist leader, had visited Stalin and discussed the possibility of the military reunification of Korea. When Mao visited Stalin later that year, Stalin mentioned Kim's military plans to him but only in very general terms. Similarly, when Kim visited Beijing in April 1950 he informed Mao of his determination to reunify his country without giving the details of any military plan or possible date of action. Mao was caught quite unawares by the North Korean invasion. He had not even had time to establish an embassy in Pyongyang, the North Korean capital.

The Chinese were obliged to use as an intermediary with the Americans a neutral party, the Indian ambassador, K.M. Pannikar. The Chinese at first had no intention of intervening in the Korean War, and were apprehensive lest the Americans use the war as an excuse to back a Guomindang invasion of China. Mao warned Kim not to overextend his troops in his rapid push southwards, and predicted that MacArthur might stage a counter-offensive through an amphibious landing near Seoul or Pyongyang. When the Inchon landing occurred on 15 September, and United Nations troops rapidly advanced towards the Chinese border, the Chinese leaders, through their Indian diplomatic channel, issued repeated calls to the Americans not to encroach on Chinese territory.

In theoretical terms, Mao had to choose between the imperialist and socialist powers. According to Peng Dehuai, 'to Mao's mind, if China stood by when North Korea was in peril, then the Soviet Union could also stand by when China was in peril; and "internationalism would be empty talk".'[21] In reality, however, the Chinese demanded more economic assistance and military aid from Stalin, who was happy to see them fight a war which would only further their international isolation.[22] Furthermore, the Chinese agreed to the continuation of Russian advisers in Port Dairen, appearing thereby to enhance Stalin's control over his Chinese neighbours. The military effectiveness of the Chinese, however, in holding their own against the full might of American military power, and their diplomatic performance at the Geneva talks on the Korean Armistice, raised Chinese international standing.

Stalin's death in 1953 ushered in a new honeymoon period between the two powers, and the Chinese leaders acted swiftly to reimpose their own control at home. In 1955 Gao Gang was expelled from the Party for trying to create an 'independent kingdom' in Manchuria, by which action the Chinese leadership was finally cleansed of Stalinist influence. The joint stock companies in Xinjiang were abandoned. Deng Xiaoping was named as General Secretary of the Party, and the draft of the Second Five Year Plan clearly reflected the desire of the Chinese leaders to get away from the heavy-industry emphasis of the First Plan.

In the international arena, China excelled itself at the Bandung Conference, where Zhou underlined the distinctive Asianness of the Chinese Communists, and ensured that the

Soviet Union was not invited even as an observer. As Mao's eulogy over the death of Stalin had stated with calculated irony, 'everyone knows that Comrade Stalin had an ardent love for the Chinese people and believed the might of the Chinese revolution to be immeasurable.'[23] But the Russian leaders, still divided between the remnants of Stalin's henchmen and a newer, more pragmatic group, were once more faced with an ominous challenge to the Soviet revolutionary line.

Khrushchev's de-Stalinization speech at a closed session of the Twentieth Congress of the Soviet Communist Party in 1956 posed new difficulties for the Chinese leaders, however. At first they did not seriously object to the de-Stalinization process, but Khrushchev's speech was the start of a new episode in this strained relationship. 'Both the things he [Stalin] did right and the things he did wrong,' a *People's Daily* editorial commented in 1956, 'were phenomena of the international Communist movement and bore the imprint of the times.'[24] By stating that Stalin's policies from 1930 to 1950 were wrong, Khrushchev brought discredit upon the world Communist movement as a whole for its behaviour during the time that the Chinese Party had come to power. For Mao, the evaluation of Stalin should not in any case be unilateral, and Khrushchev's attempts to distance the man from the system struck the Chinese leaders as absurd and potentially explosive.

The Chinese also criticized Khrushchev for his failure to 'consult with the fraternal parties in advance'.[25] According to Roy Medvedev, the anti-Stalinist Soviet historian,

it was not only Mao Zedong, but the entire generation of Communist Party leaders of the 1930s and 1940s, who were raised in the firm conviction that the world Communist movement must have a guide, and that it should be the most experienced and authoritative of the Communist parties, as well as the most authoritative, most 'wise' of all the leaders of the Communist movement.[26]

By criticizing Stalin in the way he did, and failing to consult Mao before doing so, Khrushchev (who, unlike Mao, could not claim authorship of a single work on Marxist theory) was felt by the Chinese to have undermined both parties simultaneously. It was this kind of patronizing attitude which had poisoned the relationship between the two parties from the Chinese Communist Party's inception in 1921.

Another part of Khrushchev's speech which particularly annoyed the Chinese was his theory of 'peaceful co-existence' with the capitalist countries. Khrushchev argued that Lenin's theory of continuing struggle against imperialist countries was no longer applicable in the nuclear age, and that 'we must go further, towards an improvement of relations, a strengthening of trust between them and collaboration'. The new Soviet leader's position was that 'there are only two paths: either peaceful co-existence, or the most devastating war in history. There is no third way.'[27]

In November 1957, Mao made his second and last visit to the Soviet Union to proclaim his disagreement with Khrushchev's concept of a peaceful transition to socialism. Mao's Marxist theories were based on the premise of struggle producing a better society, one which the imperialists, no matter how well-equipped militarily, would never be able to hinder. Reliance on peaceful methods of attaining socialism would serve only to 'weaken the revolutionary will of the proletariat', at the very moment that the Communist bloc, from its centre in the Soviet Union, appeared to have acquired technological superiority over the capitalist countries. Mao's claim that 'The East Wind prevails over the West Wind' referred to the successful launch of a Soviet satellite and development of thermonuclear weapons.[28] For the Chinese, the two blocs were now militarily equal, with the Communists holding the advantage because they represented the masses of the people.

Mao's references to thermonuclear war in his speech at the fortieth anniversary of the October Revolution made the Soviet leaders, who had just signed a technological defence agreement with the Chinese, nervous. 'I debated this question with a foreign statesman,' Mao recalled, in reference to a conversation he had had with Nehru.

He believed that if an atomic war was fought, the whole of mankind would be annihilated. I said that if the worst came to the worst and half of mankind died, the other half would remain while imperialism would be razed to the ground and the whole world would become socialist . . . If imperialism insists on fighting a war, we will have no alternative but to make up our minds and fight to the finish before going ahead with our construction. If every day you are afraid of war and war eventually comes, what will you do then?[29]

The Chinese Communist experience during the civil war, and, more importantly, against the might of the West during the Korean War, had made Mao believe in the ability of people to overcome any obstacles in their struggle for a socialist society.

For the remainder of 1957 both sides continued to eye each other warily, fighting ideological skirmishes in Eastern Europe, especially over the issue of Yugoslavia. Tito's intervention in the Hungarian revolt of 1956 and his vision of Yugoslavia as a role model for other countries in the Communist bloc, irritated the Chinese. They later cited Tito's Pula speech in 1956 as one of the starting points in their break with the Soviet Union. 'The Tito clique did its utmost to vilify the socialist system, insisted that "a thorough change is necessary in the political system" of Hungary, and asserted that the Hungarian comrades "need not waste their efforts on trying to restore the Communist Party".'[30]

Behind Chinese discontent with Yugoslavia, and China's later use of Albania as its puppet state in Eastern Europe, lay a tussle over the leadership of the Communist international movement. In 1963 *Red Flag* stated:

If the Communist parties maintain relations of equality among themselves and reach common understanding and take concerted action through genuine, and not nominal, exchange of views, their unity will be strengthened. Conversely, if, in their mutual relations, one party imposes its views upon others, or if the parties use the method of interference in each other's internal affairs instead of comradely suggestions and criticism, then unity will be impaired.[31]

In his speech *On the Ten Great Relationships*, Mao had given a veiled warning against Soviet arrogance in these matters. 'The victory of the People's Revolution in 1949 came over thirty years later than the Soviet October Revolution. So it is not our place to be proud. And although our revolution is one step ahead of those of a number of colonial countries, we should resist the temptation to be proud of that too.'[32] By concentrating on the continuing importance of contradictions within a socialist society, however, Mao had directly challenged orthodox Soviet interpretations of the transitionary path to Communism. In terms of the Sino–Soviet relationship, the launching of the Great Leap Forward in 1958, coupled with the sudden abandonment of the more gradualist Second Five Year Plan, appeared as a direct challenge to the development line which Moscow was endeavouring to impose on the Chinese.

The Chinese leaders, especially Mao, were simply adhering to the Sinified, and therefore nominally independent, Marxism that had enabled them to win the revolutionary war in the first place. In March 1958, after first stressing that China should be on friendly terms with the Soviet Union and should 'learn from the good points of the Soviet Union and other foreign countries', Mao once again emphasized the importance of distinctive Chinese conditions. 'There are two methods of learning: one is merely to imitate, and the other is to apply the creative spirit. Learning should be combined with creativity. To import Soviet codes and conventions inflexibly is to lack the creative spirit.'[33]

The change in the relationship between the two powers did not occur because of theoretical differences: these had existed since the Comintern's rule over the Party in the 1920s. Rather it was the emergence of the Chinese Communists on the international scene that represented a new challenge to Soviet control over the foreign policy of all Communist countries. While Stalin was at the helm, he had been largely unchallenged as leader of the Communist international movement. Khrushchev, however, was attempting to impose a new revolutionary line on the world Communist movement, which was the very antithesis of Chinese Marxist theory and experience. Mao's intensive bombing campaign against the offshore island of Quemoy, which was still held by the Guomindang, threw down a challenge to Khrushchev's theory of peaceful co-existence, and Moscow's reaction to the Chinese border dispute with its protégé India in 1959 brought these international differences out into the open.

Having ridiculed the people's communes as 'old-fashioned' and 'reactionary', Khrushchev then pilloried their creators as having 'a poor idea of what Communism is and how it is to be built'.[34] On 9 September 1959, the official Soviet news agency TASS issued a statement on the Sino–Indian border dispute, expressing 'regret' at the 'misunderstanding' that had occurred on the frontier. The Chinese could view this only as a flagrant breach of proletarian solidarity, and were angry because the Russians showed them the statement only at the last moment, and refused Chinese requests not to publish it to the world.

At the end of September, Khrushchev arrived in Beijing to defend his stand. 'We must think realistically,' he said, 'and understand the contemporary situation correctly. This, of course, does not by any means signify that if we are strong, then we must test by force the stability of the capitalist system. This would be wrong: the peoples would not understand and would never support those who would think of acting in this way.'[35]

By 1960, then, the two parties were split between Soviet 'revisionists' and Chinese 'dogmatists', and a World Conference of Communist Parties was held in Moscow in an attempt to achieve conceptual unity. Only two important party leaders were missing – Mao Zedong and Palmiro Togliatti, the Italian Secretary General, whose theories formed the basis of the revisionists' argument. Khrushchev reaffirmed his principles of peaceful co-existence and may have hoped that the presence of Liu Shaoqi and Deng Xiaoping, whose gradualist approach had by then replaced Mao's policies of continuous struggle, would help shore up party-to-party relations. But the differences over theory between the two camps remained as wide as ever. The sudden withdrawal of Soviet aid and technical advisers in July and August 1960 damaged China's economy but strengthened the collective leadership of the Chinese Communists. By withdrawing Soviet economic aid, Khrushchev had played his last card in the dispute, and Deng reaffirmed that the Chinese Communists would not be browbeaten into dependency upon the USSR.

In 1920 Lenin's arbitration between the Occidental view of Serrati and the Oriental ideas of M.N. Roy in the Comintern had been accepted because of his revolutionary credibility. In 1960, however, there was no ideologue capable or credible enough to bridge the gap between the two sides. What emerged in the final resolution was an amalgamation of the two theories, which contradicted itself throughout, and was used by both sides to justify their own theoretical position. Some parties, including the Italian, French and Polish, rallied behind Moscow because they were alarmed by the belligerence of the Chinese. Others, including the Japanese, Burmese, North Korean and Albanian, found the Chinese position closer to the original ideals of the movement. The Soviet leaders were left to rue the fact that their authority over the world Communist movement was no longer an inherited right.

With no end in sight to the dispute over theory, the two parties continued wooing fellow-Communist parties throughout the world, using Albania and Yugoslavia as the stalking horses for their arguments. Khrushchev cut relations with Albania in July 1961, leaving the Chinese to move in with economic aid and technical assistance. In October, at the Twenty-Second Congress of the Soviet Party, Zhou Enlai rebuked Khrushchev.

We consider that, if quarrels and differences of opinion have, unfortunately, arisen between the fraternal parties and fraternal countries, then they should be resolved with patience, in the spirit of equality and of reaching unity of view by means of consultation. The open, unilateral condemnation of any fraternal party does not promote cohesion. Openly to reveal in front of enemies quarrels between fraternal parties and fraternal countries cannot be regarded as a serious Marxist-Leninist approach.[36]

Khrushchev retorted that the Chinese were to blame for the Albanian Party's anti-Soviet stance, but Zhou had already left Moscow, having pointedly laid wreaths not only at Lenin's tomb but at Stalin's also. This infuriated the Soviet leaders, who promptly removed Stalin's remains from Lenin's tomb and reburied them in a simple grave outside.

By 1962, Mao was declaring explicitly, although not for open publication, that the CPSU had been usurped by 'revisionists'. He called on the Russian people to rise up and overthrow them. Mao rejected not only capitalism but also the technical rationality of capitalist systems. His emphasis on struggle as opposed to rationality, and on mass action against managerial and technical elites, went against the grain not only of Khrushchevism but even of Leninism itself. Stalin had used mass action as a political tool, but he criticized egalitarianism as a 'reactionary petty-bourgeois absurdity worthy of some primitive sect of ascetics'.[37] In Mao's eyes the Soviet leaders had lost the revolutionary élan which had brought them to power, and he echoed Bertrand Russell's feelings on visiting Russia in 1920. 'This is what I believe to be likely to happen in Russia,' Russell had said: 'the establishment of a bureaucratic aristocracy, concentrating authority in its own hands, and creating a regime just as oppressive and cruel as that of capitalism.'[38]

The sale of Soviet MIG jet fighters to India in October 1962, and Khrushchev's Cuban nuclear warhead fiasco, which the Chinese criticized initially for its 'adventurism' and then for its 'capitulationism', narrowed the possibility of a truce between the two powers. Before the final round of bilateral talks between the two parties, attended on the Chinese side by Peng Zhen and Deng Xiaoping, further recriminations sealed the fate of the relationship. Mao's thesis that the centre of the world's revolutionary struggles was to be found in the Third World, was the culmination of the Chinese desire to establish their own Marxist-Leninist credentials.

'In a sense, therefore,' the Chinese letter to the CPSU accepting the offer for bilateral talks on 14 July stated, 'the whole cause of the proletarian revolution hinges on the outcome of the revolution of the peoples of these areas, who constitute the overwhelming majority of the world's population.'[39] Ever since the Sinification of Marxism this had been the essence of Chinese Communism, and while they were willing to admit the leadership role of the Soviet Union within the Communist bloc, they were not prepared to tolerate advice which had all the hallmarks of the patronizing attitudes which the Chinese had experienced at Russian hands during their own revolution.

Following Khrushchev's fall in Russia, a Chinese delegation led by Zhou Enlai visited the new Soviet leadership. At a Kremlin reception, however, the Defence Minister, Marshal Rodion Malinovski, reportedly told a Chinese aide that, 'We have already ousted Khrushchev. You should follow our example and topple Mao.' The visit was curtailed, and the two parties broke off relations.[40]

Mao's launching of the Cultural Revolution in 1966 could be seen as a reaction to this bureaucratic attitude which he saw as the explanation for the Soviet Union's decline into 'phoney Communism'. Ironically, three of the Chinese representatives at the Sino–Soviet talks – Peng Zhen, Liu Shaoqi and Deng Xiaoping – found themselves bearing the brunt of Mao's charges of 'revisionism'. One of the three speeches of Mao which became required reading for all Chinese during the Cultural Revolution was his tract, *In Memory of Norman Bethune*, written in 1939. In this tribute to the Canadian Communist Mao praised Bethune's 'spirit of internationalism', and reproved Communists in words which were clearly directed against the Soviet leadership.

There are not a few people who are irresponsible in their work, preferring the light and shirking the heavy, passing the burdensome tasks on to others and choosing the easy ones for themselves. At every turn they think of themselves before others . . . [instead] we must all learn the spirit of absolute selflessness from him [Norman Bethune]. A man's ability may be great or small, but if he has this spirit, he is already noble-minded and pure, a man of moral integrity and above vulgar interests, a man who is of value to the people.[41]

Sino–Russian distrust harks back to the invasion of Russia by Genghis Khan in the thirteenth century, and the Tsarist expansionism in East Asia from the sixteenth century. By the end of the 1960s both sides were in full military array at the border, and fighting actually broke out at one point around the Amur river in north-eastern China. The theoretical arguments over the correct course of Marxism-Leninism had become mere expressions of vituperative contempt. The Chinese proved to the Soviets that they could exist in the international scene without their economic aid, formally following an independent foreign policy based on the struggle of the Third World. As with the Cold War between the United States and the Soviet Union, these battles were to be fought out not directly on the (Sino–Soviet) border, but in third countries around the world.[42]

The Soviet Union's invasion of Czechoslavakia in 1968, legitimized by Brezhnev in his theory of proletarian internationalism (which justified the right of one socialist country, the Soviet Union, to intervene in other socialist countries) alarmed China. As the Chinese began sounding out the possibility of détente with the United States in February 1969, the Russians took up a more threatening stance. Their Deputy Defence Minister warned in an article in *Pravda* that any war with China would certainly involve the use of nuclear weapons. On 11 September Zhou Enlai met Premier Kosygin in Beijing and agreed to open border talks with no demands for territory and a guarantee of the status quo if the talks failed. This marked the beginning of a new phase in the history of relations between the two parties, with both sides beginning realistically to accept the differences between them.

The 1970s saw the arrival of a new trilateral relationship between the USSR, the USA and China, where each power jockeyed for advantage in dealing with the others. The presence of over a million Soviet troops on China's northern border led the Chinese, however, to be more worried about the Russians than the Americans, especially when the Soviet Union began to be active in South East Asia, which had always been primarily fearful of Chinese expansionism. After the American defeat in Vietnam in 1975, the Chinese warned the Asian people against letting the 'Soviet tiger' in through the back door as the 'American wolf' left by the front. Soviet backing for the Vietnamese Communists, especially after their invasion of Cambodia in 1978, increased fears among the Chinese leaders of being surrounded by an antagonistic power. Even though the Soviet leaders made conciliatory gestures following Mao's death in 1976, their invasion of Afghanistan in 1979 heightened these fears once more.

The ideological stance which the Chinese Communists took against the Soviet Union was most vividly seen in their defiance of hegemonism – crudely defining a hegemonic superpower by the nature of its international actions, rather than in classical Marxist-Leninist terms based on socio-economic analysis. A superpower was thus described as a country which 'wants to be superior to others and, proceeding from that position of strength, to lord it over China'.[43] As the Chinese Communists took their first tentative steps back on to the international stage, this definition was refined to convey the message that the social-imperialistic actions of the Soviet Union abroad were caused by a restoration of capitalism domestically, through the usurpation of power by a bureaucratic monopoly capitalist class. As the post-Mao leadership came to terms with the continuing economic sluggishness of China's own form of socialism, however, the Chinese were obliged to recognize that the Soviet Union had reached a 'developed' or 'mature' stage of socialism compared with China's 'primary stage' model.

The ideological differences between the two parties then began to abate, and the possibilities for reconciliation appeared to grow. Hu Yaobang visited Yugoslavia in the early 1980s, and on his return appealed to Chinese peasants to learn from Yugoslavian agro-industrial complexes. Hungary was visited by other Chinese experts from the State Council, while contacts with West European Communist Parties, staunch backers of the Soviet line during the Sino–Soviet rift, also increased. In 1980, Enrico Berlinger, the Secretary General of the Italian Communist Party, visited Beijing, followed two years later by his French counterpart, Georges Marchais. The restoration of Sino–French inter-party relations was the first instance since the 1960s of the Chinese Communists' accepting inter-party relations with a dedicated supporter of the CPSU.

The barriers between the Chinese and Russian parties had crumbled with the demise of Communist ideology. The barriers between the two states, however, continued. In the early 1980s Brezhnev attempted to initiate the normalization of relations, and talks at the deputy foreign minister level were held in Beijing in October 1982. Seven months earlier, in a major foreign policy speech in Tashkent, Brezhnev had declared that

Moscow recognized China as a socialist country and indicated that ideological issues were no longer important.

For Deng, it would appear that Brezhnev was right – there were no longer major ideological differences separating the two parties. The three obstacles which Deng identified as hampering normalization – the Soviet troops on China's northern border, the Soviet forces in Afghanistan, and the Vietnamese troops in Cambodia – were specifically inter-state issues requiring the Russians to make the first move. As Deng told Utsunomiya Tokuma, the President of the Japan–China Friendship Association, in 1982, 'What we attach importance to is not words but practical actions. If there is any practical action on the part of the Soviet Union over the border issue and the question of the threat to China, talks will be continued.'[44]

As Mikhail Gorbachev rose to power in the Soviet Union, the Chinese eagerly awaited these first steps to be taken, by a man who appeared to have broken free from the military and envied the economic reforms that had been undertaken in China under Deng Xiaoping. In 1986 Gorbachev made a speech in Vladivostok addressing two out of the three Chinese demands. Six Soviet regiments were to be withdrawn from Afghanistan, troop reductions in Mongolia were announced and Gorbachev proposed reducing the number of troops along the Sino–Soviet border. Over the issue of the undelineated border, Gorbachev also offered to accept China's request that the main navigation channel along the Amur river should constitute the border. As an added incentive, Gorbachev proposed that Chinese scientists take part in the Soviet space programme.

Border negotiations were indeed resumed in 1987, after a gap of eight years, and a major economic agreement was signed which called for the five-fold increase of country-to-country trade by the beginning of the 1990s. Premier Zhao Ziyang used the example of the USSR to vindicate the general basis of his reform programme: 'At present,' he stated in 1985, 'even the Soviet Union is engaged in reform. Reform has become the tide in the socialist countries. Without reform, there is no way out.'[45] When the Soviet Party decided to rehabilitate Bukharin, who had defended the Soviet peasantry against Stalin's collectivization drive, the Chinese welcomed it. Gorbachev continued to call for a Sino–Soviet summit, following his Vladivostok speech, but Deng declined because the Vietnamese army was still in Cambodia.

By 1989 two out of the three obstacles had been firmly dealt with. At Geneva in February, the Soviets agreed to withdraw their remaining troops from Afghanistan. In December 1987, the signing of the INF agreement between the USSR and the USA had led to the elimination of Soviet SS-20s along the Sino–Soviet border. Then Vietnam agreed to withdraw forces from Cambodia, and in May Gorbachev arrived in Beijing for his long-dreamt-of Sino–Soviet summit. The Chinese leaders had already formed reservations, however, about the political policies which the Soviet leader had advanced in both his own country and the Eastern European satellites. China had troubles of its own, also, and student demonstrations spoilt the plans of Deng Xiaoping, who had spoken out so fiercely against Khrushchev in Moscow twenty-nine years earlier, to bring his Soviet counterpart finally to treat him on an equal footing.

Following the Tiananmen Square massacre, the Hungarian, Polish and Yugoslavian governments condemned the Chinese use of force, suspended Party-to-Party exchanges and cut back state-to-state traffic to a minimum. Gorbachev was careful not to get himself involved with the student demonstrations while in Beijing, but his refusal to sanction similar action against the uprisings in Eastern Europe five months later was a clear sign of his feelings. Hardliners within the Chinese leadership criticized Gorbachev for his 'subversion of socialism', while Vice Premier Wang Zhen called for China to 'go public' with its criticisms of 'Soviet revisionism'.[46]

Within Asia, however, inter-Communist party relations improved. Kim Il Sung, the veteran leader of North Korea and a skilful manipulator of Sino–Soviet differences, visited Beijing in November 1989, before Li Peng had been 'allowed' to visit Moscow (which he did in April 1990). The Chinese leaders' concern over events in Eastern Europe, and, more recently, political freedom in Mongolia, echoed the feelings of Kim, and also led to tentative contacts with the Vietnamese leadership. The old national differences remain between the Chinese and the Communist governments on their borders.

But all the Asian Communist parties are so beset by domestic problems that inter-party relations are left to simmer for a while on the back ring.

Throughout their relationship, the Chinese and Soviet Communist parties have been hindered by the national differences to which Lenin alluded in his *Left-Wing Communism – An Infantile Disorder*. By the 1980s the international scene had changed so much that Lenin's theory of imperialism, and of a Communist bloc uniting to defeat a capitalist bloc, had been effectively rejected by both Communist parties. The Chinese leaders have fluctuated between promoting Chinese-style revolution in other countries and a more pragmatic international perspective, but at least they have finally succeeded in attaining the equality with – and respect of – the Soviet Union which Mao first demanded in 1949. In the process of gaining respectability for their own national version of Marxism-Leninism, however, the Chinese leaders might also have to bear some of the responsibility for the collapse of the international Communist system.

7 *Imperialism vs. Pragmatism* –
The Question of the Superpowers:
II. USA

Before the Western imperial powers arrived in Asia, Chinese foreign policy followed a pattern of Sinocentrism resting on Confucian ideology. China perceived itself as the centre of human civilization – hence the Chinese name for their country, *Zhongguo*, literally translated as the Middle Kingdom – and the Emperor's mandate as the Son of Heaven conveyed the right to govern the affairs of all humanity. Through this theory of *Pax Sinica*, every state outside the borders of the Middle Kingdom had to acknowledge the Emperor's superiority by the ritual of paying tribute. The Emperor of China maintained his legitimacy by the practice of Confucianist ideology, with its stress on harmony in the world of the 'barbarians'. *The Doctrine of the Mean*, a Confucian canonical text, idealized this ethical approach to foreign policy.

> While there are no stirrings of pleasure, anger, sorrow, or joy, the mind may be said to be in the state of EQUILIBRIUM. When those feelings have been stirred, and they act in their due degree, there ensues what may be called the state of HARMONY. This EQUILIBRIUM is the great root *from which grow all the human actions* in the world, and this HARMONY is the universal path *which they all should pursue*.
>
> Let the states of equilibrium and harmony exist in perfection, and a happy order will prevail throughout heaven and earth, and all things will be nourished and flourish.[1]

The first Westerners to reach China's shores in any numbers were the Portuguese, who docked at Guangzhou in 1517 and were initially welcomed by the Chinese. Their rude behaviour, however, soon revived traditional Chinese fears about foreign barbarians, and subsequent Chinese attitudes towards traders from all Western countries became as stereotyped as the images brought back to Europe about inscrutable orientals. Western nations began to press the Imperial Court for diplomatic recognition on their own terms, but the court insisted upon the complete subservience of all barbarians to the Son of Heaven. Confrontation loomed between Eurocentrism and Sinocentrism.

'Are we not much superior to them [the Chinese]?' asked Griffith John in a letter to the London Missionary Society in 1869. 'Are we not more manly, more intelligent, more skilful, more human, more civilized, nay, are we not more estimable in every way? Yes, according to our way of thinking. No, emphatically no, according to theirs. And it would be nearly as difficult for us to alter our opinion on the subject as it is for them to alter theirs.'[2] In 1839 the first Opium War broke out between Britain and China, and the Imperial Court was coerced into accepting the first of the 'unequal' treaties which would provide much of the impetus for the growth of the anti-imperialist Chinese Communist Party almost eighty years later.

By the end of the nineteenth century, China had been forced by the Western powers to accept their terms of trade, and the Imperial Court was obliged to reappraise Confucianism. The Arrow War, between 1856 and 1858, and the Western military expedition to Beijing in 1860 demonstrated the ineptitude of the old-style Chinese military, and new emphasis was afterwards laid on developing a modern army and navy to combat the foreign powers. The year 1900 saw the first popular uprising against imperialism, the so-called Boxer Rebellion, sanctioned by the Empress Dowager but swiftly crushed by the Western powers. Chinese students began to look to Japan for inspiration, envying the success of the Meiji Restoration in rejuvenating Japanese society and stiffening its resistance against foreign intrusions.

Sun Yat-sen was one of the founding members of the Nationalist Party, which sought to launch revolution on the mainland. When the Emperor was toppled from his throne in 1912, however, China soon divided into regional warlord states, and the southern-based Nationalist government was unable to unite the country against foreign infiltration. Western governments preferred a disunited China, wherein they could play the warlords off against each other for their own economic benefit. Sun's disillusion with the Western powers was evident when he concluded in 1923 the famous Sun–Joffe treaty with Bolshevik Russia, which led to the reorganization of the Nationalist Party along Leninist lines, and made it a high priority to assert Chinese control over their own country.

In his seminal tract, the *San Min Chu I*, Sun listed the Chinese territories which the imperialists had snatched during the declining years of the Qing Dynasty. These ranged from Korea and Port Arthur in the east to Nepal, Burma and Ceylon in the west. 'In its age of greatest power,' Sun wrote, 'the territory of the Chinese Empire was very large, extending northward to the north of the Amur, southward to the south of the Himalayas, eastward to the China Sea, westward to the Cong Lin.' Likewise, Jiang Jieshi, Sun's successor as leader of the Nationalist Party, declared in his *China's Destiny* how 'the memory of the disastrous loss of Ryukyu, Hong Kong, Formosa [Taiwan], the Pescadores, Indo-China, Burma and Korea was still fresh . . .'[3]

Mao's claims for lost territories were actually less sweeping than those of his more right-wing contemporaries. In an interview with Edgar Snow in 1936 he declared:

It is the immediate task of China to regain all our lost territories, not merely to defend our sovereignty below the Great Wall. This means that Manchuria must be regained. We do not, however, include Korea, formerly a Chinese colony, but when we have re-established the independence of the lost territories of China, and if the Koreans wish to break away from the chains of Japanese imperialism, we will extend them our enthusiastic help in their struggle for independence. The same applies for Formosa. As for Inner Mongolia, which is populated by both Chinese and Mongolians, we will struggle to drive Japan from there and help Inner Mongolia to establish an autonomous state.[4]

Indeed, while Lenin's theories of imperialism played such an important role in the growth of Chinese Communism, the personal experience of many Chinese Communist leaders counteracted any desire to regain the former Chinese empire. One of the most formative experiences during the growth of the Party was the massacre of Communist cadres and their supporters in Shanghai in 1927. Before Jiang's triumphant Northern Expeditionary Army entered the city, he had held talks with the American 'Lord Mayor' of the International Community, Sterling Fessenden, and with Pat Givens, the Irish chief of the political department of the Shanghai International Settlement Police. While wanting to deliver a decisive blow to the Communists within his Party, Jiang also wanted to break free of the Sun–Joffe agreement, which had left the Nationalist Party reliant on Russian funds, and thus break free from Russian influence.

For Western traders in Shanghai, the spectre of expropriation under Communism was a real threat. Sterling and Fessenden offered Jiang 5,000 rifles, armoured cars and safe conduct through the nominally 'neutral' International Concessions, in return for destroying the 'commune' in the Chinese city and a monthly fee to various officials for the continued passage of opium through the French concession. With this backing, and the help of the local secret society leader, Du Yuesheng, Jiang was able to catch the Communist leaders off guard. Between five and ten thousand workers were executed. Zhou Enlai, later to become the Premier of the People's Republic, narrowly escaped arrest.[5]

For the next six years, the Communists were under constant attack in their underground lairs in Shanghai, and had to relocate their revolutionary struggle in the countryside. Even here, however, they were not safe from Jiang and his foreign advisers. During the five encirclement campaigns against the Jiangxi soviet, from 1930 to 1934, German generals helped Jiang to formulate his military strategy which eventually forced the Communists to undertake the Long March. By the time the Red Army reached its new base in the north of the country, China faced a new imperialist threat in the shape of the Japanese. Under Mao's general theory of contradictions, the Japanese invasion of China now became the principal contradiction which the Chinese Communists would have to tackle first.

Throughout the Sino–Japanese War, which merged with the Pacific War and Second World War in 1941, the Chinese Communists adopted a united front stance against the Japanese, allying themselves for that purpose with the United States, Britain and France. The Americans viewed the Chinese struggle against Japan with sympathy, giving arms and military advice to Jiang's government. From across the Pacific, the nascent China Lobby in America promoted the Chinese struggle as a fraternal movement, and Jiang's wife, Song Meiling, delivered stirring speeches to raise funds for the Guomindang government. In China itself, however, American enthusiasm was less fervent. The corruption and back-stabbing factionalism there raised serious doubts in the minds of some State Department officials over America's choice of Chinese partner.

The US State Department first came into contact with the Chinese Communists in 1944, with the arrival of the 'Dixie Mission' at the Yan'an base in north China. Before meeting them Mao told his Central Committee how important it was to forge links with the Americans. The Central Committee's conclusion, published in *On Diplomatic Work*, was that 'the Allies should be received warmly and modestly. It is necessary to refrain from excessive luxury while avoiding indifference.'[6] A week later Mao gave his first interview to John Service, the China expert in the US group, in a room where portraits of Roosevelt and Churchill hung beside those of Stalin and Lenin.

'Basic to all these problems, the Communists believe, are the policies and actions of the United States,' Service wrote in a memorandum to his seniors in Washington after the interview.

> We can, if we wish, prevent civil war and force the Guomindang toward democracy. These American policies will decide whether the Communists must play a lone hand and look out for themselves, or whether they can be assured of survival and participation in a democratic China, and so co-operate wholeheartedly in the war. The Communists want our understanding and support: they are anxious to do nothing to alienate us or compromise that support.[7]

Mao continued to underline the importance of American support for the Communists in their struggle against the Japanese, and in the post-war make-up of China. 'Even the most conservative American businessman can find nothing in our programme to take exception to,' he boasted to Service regarding the Communist land reform policies. 'America does not need to fear that we will not be co-operative. We must co-operate and we must have American help . . . We cannot risk crossing you – cannot risk any conflict with you.'[8] On 9 January 1945, Mao told the Dixie Mission that he and Zhou Enlai were ready to go to Washington to meet President Roosevelt in person. Unfortunately for Mao, his request for complete secrecy with the message was not heeded. The American Ambassador to the Guomindang government, through whom the message was channelled, was able to read in it that the Communist leaders did not trust his discretion, and so he delayed sending it on to Washington.

Mao kept trying. He told Service:

between the people of China and the people of the United States there are strong ties of sympathy, understanding and mutual interest. Both are essentially democratic and individualistic. Both are by nature peace-loving, non-aggressive and non-imperialistic . . . For all these reasons there must not and cannot be a conflict, estrangement or misunderstanding between the Chinese people and America . . .[9]

In his final interview before Service was recalled to Washington, Mao stated that, 'America is not only the most suitable country to assist this economic development of China, she is also the only country able to participate.'[10] Yet five years later, Chinese Communist troops and American soldiers were fighting each other on the Korean battlefield.

After the defeat of Japan the United States had tried to mediate between the two warring Chinese sides, but went on funding the Guomindang, much to the Communists' pique. During this period, from 1945 to 1949, as the Americans became deeply embroiled in Chinese politics, the Communist leaders gradually fell back on their second option of a 'one-sided' policy of leaning towards Moscow. 'The United States,' Mao wrote in bitter sarcasm on the eve of the establishment of the People's Republic, 'supplies the money and guns and Jiang Jieshi the men to fight for the United States and slaughter the Chinese people, to "destroy the Communists" and turn China into a US colony, so that the United States may fulfil its "international responsibilities" and carry out its "traditional policy of friendship for China".'[11]

By continuing to underwrite the Guomindang, Mao argued, the Americans had failed to match their anti-imperialist rhetoric with deeds. This led to his famous dictum about the atomic bomb being a 'paper tiger'; Mao rejected the invincibility of a country with the A-bomb, because in his experience the most important factor in war was the popular will. While the Guomindang might draw from the mightiest military arsenal in the world, they would still lose the civil war because the people supported the Communists. 'We have only millet plus rifles to rely on, but history will finally prove that our millet plus rifles is more powerful than Jiang Jieshi's aeroplanes plus tanks,' Mao said in 1946. 'Although the Chinese people still face many difficulties and will long suffer hardships from joint attacks of US imperialism and the Chinese reactionaries, the day will come when these reactionaries are defeated and we are victorious. The reason is simply this: the reactionaries represent reaction, we represent progress.'[12]

After they had defeated the Guomindang in 1949, the Communists continued their strident public verbal attacks on their foe's American backers. Behind the scenes, however, economic necessity and their yearning to have some degree of independence from Moscow prompted the Communists to make informal approaches to US representatives in China. Ambassador Stuart Leighton, during his last days on the mainland, wrote that 'according to my friends in Beijing, Mao openly stated that I would be welcomed in Beijing', and 'counted on entertaining me and talking to me during this ostensibly private visit to Beijing'.[13] In December, the US Consul General in Shanghai informed the State Department that Madame Sun Yat-sen, acting as a representative of the Chinese Communists, would be willing to meet the Ambassador-at-Large, Philip Jessup, during his visit to Hong Kong.[14] 'Of course we will lean to one side,' the Chinese explained in another message. 'But how far depends on you.'[15]

In his *On the People's Democratic Dictatorship* Mao reiterated the official Communist policy towards the opening of diplomatic relations with other countries, which had also been included in Article 56 of the Organic Law.

> We are willing to discuss with any foreign government the establishment of diplomatic relations on the basis of equality, mutual benefit and mutual respect for territorial integrity and sovereignty, provided it is willing to sever relations with the Chinese reactionaries, stops conspiring with them or helping them, and adopts an attitude of genuine and not hypocritical, friendship towards People's China.[16]

It was therefore up to the Western powers to prove that they were willing to dissociate themselves from the Guomindang, and thus stop acting in an imperialist manner towards China. The Chinese Communists, on coming to power, had a view of the international world that was essentially a product of their internal experience: the function of foreign policy was to unite internal and external allies against any external threat. During 1949 and 1950 the main threat to China's internal affairs continued to come from the United States.

In November 1948, Harry Truman had unexpectedly been re-elected to the White House, and when Dean Acheson took office as his third Secretary of State in January 1949, China was not of primary importance in the new administration's diplomacy. But the division of Europe into two satellite blocs and the onset of the Cold War between the United States and Russia appeared to be replicated on the Asian continent by the victory of the Chinese Communists. The US administration was lambasted for its 'loss' of China. A year before the Communist victory, John Fairbank had warned his fellow-Americans that 'the greatest error Americans can make is to look at China but think only of Russian expansion. If we let ourselves become obsessed with power politics in our approach to China, we will be disastrously defeated in our policy there.'[17]

Three days after Ambassador Stuart had been officially withdrawn from China the State Department published a White Paper to demonstrate to its critics that the downfall of the Guomindang was solely to be blamed on the deficiencies of Jiang's government. This devastating blow to the Nationalists was followed by a US decision to withhold any more aid to Jiang after February 1950. Acheson was cleaning all the cobwebs out of the cupboard and leaving the American government free to recognize the People's Republic when it would be most beneficial for the White House.

Acheson hoped that such recognition would come as a united response on the part of the Western governments, something which had become more important after the successful testing of a Soviet atomic bomb in September 1949. Like the British, the Americans had to come to terms with the growth of Asian nationalism, and they had come to accept in particular the importance of the Chinese market for Japan's economic reconstruction. As Premier Yoshida Shigeru stated in 1949, 'I don't care whether China is red or green. China is a natural market, and it has become necessary for Japan to think about markets.'[18] On the other hand, Acheson faced the growing spectre of McCarthyism, led by the powerful China Lobby into blaming the State Department (especially the Dixie Mission) for the 'loss' of China in the first place.[19]

For the British government the question of recognition was more straightforward. A Foreign Office minute in December 1949 argued against the stand of the United States in 'awarding' recognition to the People's Republic; 'to insist on such an explicit statement has its disadvantages because it opens the way to the argument that the new regime is only bound by the previous obligations of the country if it expressly says it will be'.[20] More germane, perhaps, was the UK attitude towards Asian, and, in particular, Indian nationalism. 'Whereas they [the Asian nationalists] have so far co-operated with our colonial governments,' Sir Gladwyn Jebb of the British Foreign Office concluded after the Bukit Serene Conference in November in Singapore, 'their loyalties will be divided if we remain hostile to the Chinese Communist government and refuse to recognize it.'[21] On 16 December a Foreign Office memo recorded that 'the decision to accord *de jure* recognition in principle had been taken by Cabinet this morning'.[22]

Having lost the impact of a united allied stance towards the Chinese, the Americans appeared to move away from the theory that Mao was a Stalinist puppet. 'We observe gathering antipathy here [in China] toward Soviets, and Department may wish [to] hold off discussions with Chinese Communists re *de facto* recognition until possible Sino–Soviet breach becomes more noticeable,' a State Department message noted in 1949.[23] The Voice of America and official US speeches highlighted the imperialistic tendencies of the Soviet Union, in the hope of stirring up Chinese nationalism and accelerating a Sino–Soviet split. Acheson found, however, that he could not recognize the new government even if he wanted to, because of the pressures of domestic politics.

On 5 January 1950, Truman announced that the US

has no desire to obtain special rights or privileges or to establish military bases on Formosa [Taiwan] at this time. Nor does it have any intention of utilizing its armed forces to interfere in the present situation. The United States will not pursue a course which will lead to involvement in the civil conflict in China. Similarly, the United States will not provide military aid or advice to Chinese forces in Formosa.[24]

Taiwan was effectively positioned outside the defensive perimeter of the US in the Pacific, indicating to the Chinese Communists that the United States would not intervene if, and when, the Red Army launched their attack on this last-ditch Guomindang stronghold.

In February, however, pro-Nationalist sympathizers in Congress forced Truman to extend the China Aid Act from 15 February to 30 June. Contrary to the previous pledges of the government, Jiang Jieshi would receive a further $104 million in military aid.[25] Towards the end of May and the beginning of June, the decision was taken at the highest levels of the administration to defend Taiwan by force in line with the National Security Council's decision in April to meet Communism with force. When the Korean War opened on 25 June 1950, the last hopes for Sino–American rapprochement appeared to sink as the American Seventh Fleet sailed into the Taiwan Straits to defend the Guomindang government from any possible Communist attack.

During 1949, as each approach to the Americans was rebuffed, Mao began planning for the possibility of American intervention in China by hastening the process of victory, and occupying the big sea ports where large numbers of troops were stationed as a deterrent to American intervention. Rehabilitating the economy was also given high priority in case of a United States embargo. And People's Liberation Army soldiers were urged not to antagonize foreigners, so that the United States would have no excuse for intervention.

The evidence shows that the Chinese leaders were as unprepared for the Korean War as their American counterparts. Five days earlier, the decision had been taken for economic reasons to demobilize almost 30 per cent of the People's Liberation Army; when the war began, there was only one Chinese army along the Yalu river border, stationed there for crop-production purposes and to rest after the travails of the Manchurian campaign. Initially, the Chinese had no intention of intervening, reckoning to provide the North Koreans only with moral support, but Truman's despatch of the Seventh Fleet into the Taiwan Straits was perceived as 'armed aggression against Chinese territory', and the leaders became convinced that the Americans' next step would be to back the Guomindang in a resumed civil war.

Even after General MacArthur landed at Inchon on 15 September, Mao still hoped to avoid involvement in the war, though Zhou Enlai launched a diplomatic effort, via the Indian ambassador, K.M. Pannikar, to warn the United States that 'the Chinese people . . . will not simply tolerate seeing their neighbours being savagely invaded by the imperialists'.[26] On 2 October Zhou told Pannikar that if the United Nations forces moved into North Korea, China would intervene. Acheson and Truman responded with disbelief, questioning Zhou's authority to make such a threat. Further messages via Pannikar, Nehru and Ernest Bevin gave notice that if the United Nations forces should pass the 38th parallel, the original demarcation line between North and South Korea after the end of the Second World War, the Chinese would intervene.

When the UN forces continued to march north, Zhou revealed an even greater degree of apprehension among the leaders in Beijing. 'From the information we got,' he said, 'they wanted to calm China first and after occupying North Korea, they will come to attack China.'[27] When General MacArthur paid a tactless visit to Taiwan, and boasted of the possible use of Guomindang troops in the United Nations army, China could hardly avoid entering the war. According to the historians Hao Yufan and Zhai Zhihai, 'Mao was forced to enter the war by the situation created by the United States government. His decision was based on a choice of the least dangerous of his limited options.'[28]

The effect of the Korean War on Sino–American relations cannot be overestimated. Just when the Communists desperately needed peace and stability, following twenty-two years of civil war, they were once again faced by the direct threat of aggressive imperialism aimed at their industrial heartland. The loss of over 360,000 Chinese People's 'volunteers', including a son of Mao, effectively wrecked any chance of a workable Sino–American relationship and became yet another heroic episode in the sequence of Communist struggles against imperialism in China. As John Service had written in 1944, 'The Party's twenty-three years of almost continuous struggle and war have not only affected the attitudes and character of its leaders, they have also helped to determine the type of men who could survive and rise to leadership. It is difficult to understand these men without this background.'[29]

In ideological terms, the Korean War proved Mao's theory that the atomic bomb was just a 'paper tiger', and that the Chinese people, through the leadership of the Chinese Communist Party, could successfully stand up to the imperialist countries. In terms of Mao's theory of contradictions, the United States was now the primary contradiction in China's foreign policy, and was therefore to be struggled against, just as the Party had had to struggle against first the Japanese and then the Guomindang before the victory of 1949. Central to this principle of protracted conflict is Mao's axiom that the enemy should be despised strategically but respected tactically. Thus, a step-by-step process of ideological struggle followed the Korean War, as the Chinese, in the limited international arenas open to them, notably the Korean Armistice talks and the Afro-Asian Bandung Conference, mouthed rigidly anti-American rhetoric.

These tactics were intended to turn China's relative weakness on the international scene into a position of strength through notional equality. The term 'paper tiger' is thus used in a strategic sense. 'Imperialism and all reactionaries,' Mao told his Central Committee colleagues in 1958, 'looked at in essence, from a long-term point of view, from a strategic point of view, must be seen for what they are – paper tigers. On this we should build our strategic thinking. On the other hand, they are also living tigers, iron tigers, real tigers which can eat people. On this we should build our tactical thinking.'[30]

At the dialectical level Mao made no distinction between the two concepts of peace and war. They were part of the unity of opposites, each contradicting the other. One of the ideological reasons behind the Sino–Soviet split was Mao's antagonism towards the United States, and his apparent willingness to launch a full-scale nuclear war against the imperialist aggressor. Actually his concern was not so much about abstract conceptions of war and peace, but who was using violence against whom, in what sociopolitical context, and for what purpose.

As Mao explained in an editorial, *Long Live Leninism*, believed to be penned by him in 1960,

> In capitalist countries, bourgeois war is the continuation of the bourgeois policies of ordinary times, while bourgeois peace is the continuation of bourgeois wartime policy. The bourgeoisie are always switching back and forth between the two forms, war and peace, to carry on their rule over the people and their external struggle. In what they call peace time, the imperialists rely on armed force to deal with the oppressed classes and nations by such forms of violence as arrest, imprisonment, sentencing to hard labour, massacre, and so forth, while at the same time, they also carry on preparations for using the most acute form of violence – war – to suppress the revolution of the people at home, to

carry out plunder abroad, to overwhelm foreign competitors and to stamp out revolutions in other countries. Or, peace at home may exist side by side with war abroad.[31]

The Korean War reinforced the Chinese Communists' belief in the unilinear development of history, where the final struggle between capitalism and socialism was inevitable. By the late 1950s, however, the major contradiction in Chinese foreign policy had become the 'revisionist' policies of the Soviet Union, which posed a more serious threat to China than the capitalist countries did. While the attacks on the Russians in the 1960s and the Americans in the 1950s were similar in their bellicosity, the fundamental difference remained that the United States was the chief enemy because it was the leading capitalist and imperialist country, committed to halting world revolutionary movements. This enmity between the two countries would not be resolved quickly, but, as the pattern of the civil war had showed, over a period of many decades during which periods of peace and even collaboration would occur, comparable to the united front policies with the Guomindang between 1921–7 and 1936–45.

The fundamentally antagonistic nature of the relationship remained the same. Thus, in September 1962, the Chinese Communists still saw imperialism as the main enemy, but significantly defined the contradiction between the 'people of the whole world and imperialism' as the primary one. The contradiction between 'socialism and imperialism' was at the end of the list, well after the contradictions between the 'people of all countries and revisionism'.[32] Mao's attempts to formulate a foreign policy in which China remained both revolutionary and independent had not been able to flourish under the two-bloc model, and by 1962 he began formulating the theory of Three Worlds. Here, the peoples of the world were confronted with the twin dangers of imperialism and social-imperialism, and it was only through the uprisings of the peoples of Latin America, Africa and Asia that the world revolutionary movement could flourish.

This did not mean that the Chinese Communists turned their backs on the situation in the industrialized countries of the West. Unlike the structuralist approach of Togliatti, Mao argued that the morally vacuous Western proletariat should be stirred up through the revolutionary actions of a proletarian vanguard, until they began to behave as they ought to under Marxist doctrine. The 'united front from above' policy was followed with capitalist countries seeking to establish their own form of independence within the international two-bloc order. Thus, in the early 1960s, the Chinese Communists were forced to look to both the Japanese and to the Western Europeans, to the Second World, for technological imports.

They did not abandon the possibility of revolutionary struggle within these countries, but limited their support to the essentially theoretical and moral – as with the Japanese Communist Party and splinter groups of French and other Euro-Marxists, for example. As Mao declared in 1965, 'China gave support to revolutionary movements but not by sending troops. Of course, whenever a liberation struggle existed, China would publish statements and call demonstrations to support it. It was precisely that which vexed the imperialists.'[33] Two years earlier Mao had shown his support of the civil rights movement in the United States, by stating that, 'It is only the reactionary ruling clique among the whites which is oppressing the Negro people. They can in no way represent the workers, farmers, revolutionary intellectuals, and other enlightened persons who comprise the overwhelming majority of the white people.'[34]

While the Chinese leaders positioned China within the Third World, they were not willing to present themselves as leaders of a new international revolution. Instead, they promoted revolutionary ideals by advertising the failures of the United States in South East Asia and the USSR in Eastern Europe, and praising the rise of Palestinian resistance and the New Left in Europe. As Lin Biao's *Long Live the People's War* reiterated in 1965, 'the liberation of the masses is accomplished by the masses themselves – this is a basic principle of Marxism-Leninism. Revolution or people's war in any country is the business of the masses in that country, and should be carried out primarily by their own efforts; there is no other way.'[35]

The withdrawal of all Chinese ambassadors in 1967, and the consequent decline in the importance of diplomacy in favour of contacts with nominally independent revolutionary movements in the West can be seen as an attempt by the Chinese leaders to break down the bipolarity of international relations. This harmonized with Mao's launching of the Cultural Revolution, which reinforced China's revolutionary credentials. The slogan 'the Cultural Revolution is shaking the world' was often expressed, but the Chinese Communists failed to ignite the world revolutionary movement because they could not counter the propaganda of the United States and the USSR, and because the independent revolutionary movements were not united.

Another important factor in this promotion of an independent model of revolution was the threat perceived by the Chinese leaders from both the United States, which was becoming more involved in the Vietnam War, and the Soviet Union, with its build-up of forces along China's northern border. By labouring the possibility of invasion of China by the two superpowers, Mao emphasized the importance of continuing the revolutionary struggle, so that the people would still be able to defeat the 'paper tigers'. The Chinese should not respond by promoting revolutionary struggle through expansion and colonization of their immediate neighbours, because that would make them no better than the 'revisionists' in the Soviet Union.

In a speech to the First Plenum of the heavily military-dominated Ninth Central Committee in 1969, Mao reaffirmed this defensive stance:

> Others may come and attack us but we shall not fight outside our borders. We do not fight outside our borders. I say we will not be provoked. Even if you invite us to come out, we will not come out, but if you should come and attack us we will deal with you . . . They [the enemies] would be easy to fight, since they would fall into the people's encirclement.[36]

As the threat from the Soviet Union increased, however, the Chinese leaders were forced to reappraise their international situation. The first important step in this process was the admittance of the People's Republic delegation to the United Nations in 1971, through the concerted effort of the independent African countries, which brought the Chinese Communists for the first time into the international diplomatic framework. As a consequence, Mao became less bellicose towards the existing international order, though the moralistic stance of the Chinese Communists continued. In their first confrontation in a plenary session of the United Nations Security Council, the Chinese delegate, Qiao Guanhua, eloquently lectured Josef Malik, the Russian delegate, on the hegemonistic approach of the two superpowers.

> The Soviet approach towards the Chinese delegation is exactly the same as the crude behaviour towards the Afro-Asian countries adopted by another superpower not long ago. The Soviet representatives have probably become used to acting the patriarch within their small realm, and they consider that whatever they say others will have to obey. Otherwise they will label you anti-Soviet. Distinguished representatives of the Soviet Union, you are wrong. This is not anti-Sovietism; this is opposition to your attitude of Great Power chauvinism and your policies of social imperialism. We have had long experience with such behaviour of yours. The Chinese people do not buy such stuff of yours, and your baton no longer works. The days are gone when the superpowers could dominate the world.[37]

The menace of the Soviet Union build-up along China's borders, and the American intervention in Vietnam and Cambodia continued in the early 1970s to constitute the primary contradiction in China's foreign policy. Coupled with the decline of Lin Biao's doctrine of worldwide revolution within the Chinese leadership, these developments provoked a reassessment of Sino–American relations. Following a series of cultural and sporting exchanges, President Nixon became in 1972 the first American leader to have any direct contact with the Chinese Communists, though it was not until 1978 that the United States officially recognized the People's Republic, abandoning its 'two Chinas' policy.

Chinese leaders did not cease their homilies on the importance of the fight against imperialism, but the hostility from the Soviet Union and the American actions in Vietnam both broadly echoed the fears of the Chinese leaders and drove them into greater pragmatism. Answering Soviet criticism of China's new approach to Western capitalist countries in 1975, Qiao Guanghua, the chief Chinese delegate to the United Nations, remarked that, 'It seems as if this is very contradictory; in fact there is nothing contradictory about this. It is only a matter of time. In talking about situations, the most important thing is not to depart from the concept of time.'[38]

Another example of the Chinese leaders' pragmatic approach to the imperialist powers can be seen in their attitude towards Hong Kong and Macau. During the Sino–Soviet split the Chinese were criticized by the Russian comrades for failing to 'liberate' the two imperialist enclaves. 'With regard to the outstanding issues [Hong Kong and Macau], which are a legacy from the past,' a *People's Daily* editorial replied in 1963, 'we have always held that, when conditions are ripe, they should be settled peacefully through negotiations and that, pending a settlement, the status quo should be maintained.'[39] Rather than risk losing all the economic benefits from both of these 'lost territories', the Chinese Communists have preferred to take their time before resuming sovereignty of both Hong Kong and Macau.

As the two superpowers moved into a new era of détente, many Western commentators saw China reverting to its 'traditional' foreign policy of playing one barbarian off against another. In reality, however, it was the hegemonism of all imperialism, whether capitalist or state bureaucratic, that was the nexus around which Chinese foreign policy revolved. Thus, during the Gang of Four era, when Deng Xiaoping was removed from office for the second time in his career, he was not attacked for his foreign policy views, which were close to Mao's Third World theory. Similarly, in 1977, stung by the criticism of China's old protégé, the Albanian Communist Party, the *People's Daily* printed an article entitled *Chairman Mao's Theory of the Differentiation of the Three Worlds is a Major Contribution to Marxism-Leninism*. This reaffirmed that the two superpowers were the common enemies of mankind, and that the Third World was the main force against imperialism, colonialism and hegemonism, leaving the Second World as a force that could be united with in the broadest possible international united front against superpower hegemony.

In response to the charge that China was overplaying the danger of the Soviet Union to the world revolution in order to serve its own national interests, the editorial argued that because the Soviet Union was a newcomer among the imperialist countries it was more dissatisfied with the status quo, and was thus more expansionary and adventurous. Second, it argued that the Soviet Union had to rely more on war and military means for global expansion because of its relatively backward economy and technology. Third, the Russian ruling class had already transformed the Soviet economy and state organization into a highly centralized and militaristic machine.

A year later the Chinese signed with the Fukuda government a Sino–Japanese Peace and Friendship Treaty, which included an anti-hegemony clause. The joint Sino–American communiqué which followed the establishment of diplomatic relations the same year similarly reaffirmed the principle of anti-hegemony. These events marked the beginning of a pseudo-alliance between China, America and Japan, but did not end Chinese insistence on the continuing struggle against imperialism. Deng's 'Middle Kingdom' policy, which he had advocated since 1973, called for an 'even-handed' treatment of Washington and Moscow, with no leaning to either side. As long as the Soviet Union was seen as the greater threat, however, links with the United States, even to the extent of hosting CIA listening stations in northern China, intensified – until Ronald Reagan was elected to the White House in 1980.

Reagan's election pledge to revive Taiwan–American relations, and the close links between some of his senior staff members and the Guomindang alarmed the Chinese leaders, though things were patched up by a joint communiqué in 1982 reaffirming American pledges not to increase arms sales to the Taiwan government. Differences over Poland and Korea, and the protectionist policies of the Reagan administration towards Chinese textile exports also hindered state-to-state relations. These differences, coming on top of Third World allegations of China having a 'strategic relationship' with the United

States, led to Hu Yaobang's criticizing in 1981 the twin evils of hegemonism (the USSR) and imperialism (the USA).

Deng's open-door policies, however, necessitated a reappraisal of capitalism, thereby hinting at a change in attitude towards imperialism. In 1974, the Minister of Foreign Trade, Li Qiang, had boasted that China would 'never go in for joint-management with foreign countries, still less grovel for foreign loans as does that superpower [the USSR]'.[40] Yet in the 1980s, China joined the World Bank and the International Monetary Fund, and applied to join the GATT. By April 1987 China's foreign debt had soared to US $20 billion, and China for its part had invested US $477 million in 277 joint ventures in over fifty countries. Sino–American trade multiplied two and a half times between 1983 and 1988, and the United States investment in joint ventures in China, estimated at around $2.6 billion in 1989, made it the second largest foreign investor in the People's Republic.[41]

In 1982 Hu Yaobang and Zhao Ziyang both explained that China's modernization would require a peaceful international environment, and while the struggle against imperialism was still a main theme, the prospect of a broad united front, involving countries from both the Third and Second Worlds, against hegemonism, was no longer stressed. Indeed, in 1980 Hu Yaobang had gone as far as to say that an imperialist war could be 'postponed or even prevented'.[42] The fact that China was a socialist country, it was argued, made it even more necessary for it to join the world market; the self-reliance model of Mao, restricting Chinese economic growth within its own domestic boundaries, would be a 'fetter upon the productive forces'. China's independence continued to be laboured, however, in rebuttal of accusations that it was giving up the revolutionary struggle. 'In the thirty-three years since the founding of our People's Republic,' Hu Yaobang argued in 1982, 'we have shown the world by deeds that China never attaches itself to any big power or group of powers and never yields to pressures from any big power.'[43]

In 1983, the Chinese leaders changed their tack regarding the role of the Second World, taking a much more realistic view of the international economic order. Zhao Ziyang, in

a speech to the Sixth National People's Congress, declared
that 'China appreciates and supports the efforts made by West
European countries to strengthen their unity, and the positive
role they have played in international affairs.'[44] China then
began to discriminate positively in economic policy, cultivating
economic ties with the European Community, for example in
the move by the Bank of China and China International Trust
and Investment Corporation to issue bonds on the Eurodollar
market.

In 1986, Premier Zhao Ziyang pronounced China's ten principles for foreign policy, which reaffirmed Mao's five principles
of peaceful co-existence, adding those of defending world peace,
opposing hegemonism and supporting the Third World, and
reiterating the Chinese position on arms control, the open door
and support for the United Nations. It was further stated that
China's position on international issues 'would be guided by
the criteria of defending world peace, developing relationships
of friendship and co-operation among various countries and
promoting international prosperity', regardless, it appeared, of
their social system or ideology.[45]

In the following year, Zhao reaffirmed this policy in an
address to the fifth session of the Sixth National People's
Congress. 'China's socialist modernization . . . requires a stable
international environment of enduring peace . . . Maintaining
independence, China will not enter into alliances with the
superpowers, and it will endeavour to establish and expand
friendly relations and co-operation with all countries on the
basis of the Five Principles of Peaceful Co-existence.'[46]

The deradicalization of China's foreign policy occurred,
therefore, because of the necessities of its economic modernization, and because of the Chinese leaders' perception of
the international order as being stable and enduring. China
had acquired a 'fair and proper place' within that order, from
which it could pursue an independent policy line, untainted by
superpower politics.

The durability of the threat of imperialism, however, and
its use by the Chinese leaders as an ideological weapon, were
seen after the Tiananmen Square massacre of 1989. When the
Group of Seven leading industrial countries, meeting in June

1989, issued a statement condemning the massacre, the *People's Daily* editorialized:

> The problem arises simply because certain countries, out of their own likes and dislikes and their concept of values, have directly and extensively damaged China's interests and dignity with words and deeds. Any action that aims to meddle in China's internal affairs will be of no avail. The Chinese government and people will never give in to any pressure, whatever its form and whichever nation it may come from.[47]

Chinese Communist ideology has emphasized one thing above all its theoretical criticisms of imperialism, capitalism, hegemonism and social-imperialism, and that is that Chinese foreign policy would be decided by the Chinese leaders themselves, and would be independent of the Eurocentric values which prevailed in the international order in 1949. To this extent, China's joining the United Nations and the major bodies of the international capitalist economic order, has allowed it to take a moral stance towards world problems, while criticizing the imperialist attitudes of the two superpowers. Contradictions still play an important part in the formulation of foreign policy, with the evils of hegemonism still being stressed by, for example, Li Peng in 1990. But the promotion of struggle against antagonistic contradictions, or against the imperialist countries, has been dropped in favour of a more gradual and pragmatic approach.

8 *Conclusion* –
The Future of Contradictions

The primary concern of the Chinese Communists in and out of government has always been the salvation and rebirth of the Chinese nation – to result in a society based not on the principles of Confucianism, which was reponsible for China's decline, but on the tenets of a European doctrine, Marxism-Leninism. These, therefore, are the two immutable aims of Chinese Communism – to produce a society that is both Marxist, in that it formally represents and promotes the people's dignity and livelihood, and Chinese, in that it is run without foreign interference.

Some Western commentators therefore label Chinese Communism as 'Leninist Confucianism', to rub in the authoritarian and reactionary nature of the Chinese Party. Neither term is appropriate, however, to explain Chinese Communism, and put together they are positively unhelpful. Confucianism insisted upon the importance of the family over the collective, whereas Chinese Communism idealizes the collective Chinese nation, state or society. Confucianism protected the privacy of the individual, where Chinese Communism stresses his or her public duties.

The ethos of Confucianism was one of harmony – between ruler and ruled, between father and son, between China and the barbarian countries. By contrast, Chinese Communism pursues the ethic of struggle as the essential means of development. This is not only one of the elemental criteria of Mao Zedong Thought, but can be seen in the ideas of all shades of Chinese Communist thinker. Liu Shaoqi, whose dismissal symbolized the consequences of this emphasis on struggle, wrote in his *How to be a Good Communist* that, 'when Heaven is about to confer a great office on any man, it first exercises his mind with suffering, and his sinews and bones with toil.'[1] How have these two determinants of ideology – Chineseness and Communism – interacted to produce a system of government that controls the destinies of over a fifth of the world's population?

Examination of the philosophical basis of Chinese Communism, particularly its stress on contradictions, shows that when Marxism-Leninism was not ideally suited to the situation existing in China, the Chinese leaders have been forced to work within the boundaries of the existing social framework.

In another sense, Chineseness and Communism are both contradictory elements within this ideology, constantly interacting to produce some form of unity of opposites. Within the political sphere, Chinese Communism has wavered between a desire for democracy, on the one hand, and the centralizing tendencies of all one-party states on the other. Within the economy, Chinese Communism has fostered individual initiative without fully relinquishing the controls of the state plan. Within society as a whole, Chinese Communism prefers political conformity to technical brilliance. Yet the ultimate aim of this ideology's zig-zagging course has been consistent: the gradual creation of a new, strong, socialist China.

In promoting a new culture, Chinese Communism has succeeded in toppling the old trinity of Confucianism, the gentry and the paterfamilias. As the ideological purity, and popular credibility, of the Party has declined, however, so the Chinese Communists have sought to legitimize their position within society by reverting to the traditional concept of loyalty. As Richard Solomon comments, 'the "dialectic" in China's national development [is] not the conflict of classes but the tension between established patterns of culture and personality, and the new values and behavioural norms'.[2] In one area in particular, that of the continuation of what has been labelled 'Emperor-ism' – or veneration for the top leader – Chinese Communism has failed to break with tradition.

The concept of the leader being the source of correct doctrine is deeply rooted in both Leninist theory and Chinese tradition. In March 1958, Mao Zedong noted:

There are two kinds of cult of the individual. One is correct, such as that of Marx, Engels, Lenin, and the correct side of

Stalin. These we ought to revere and continue to revere for ever . . . As they held the truth in their hands, why should we not revere them? . . . A squad should revere its squad leader; it would be quite wrong not to. Then there is the incorrect cult of the individual in which there is no analysis, simply blind obedience. This is not right.[3]

But who will judge the judges and discern correctness?

The Cultural Revolution appeared to epitomize this 'blind obedience' to the Great Leader, Mao Zedong. The cult of Mao can be traced not just to the 1945 Congress of Victors, when Mao Zedong Thought first appeared within the Party Constitution, but to the point, in 1927, when the Chinese Communists were forced to readapt their theories to suit Chinese conditions. It was during that time that the myth of the infallibility of Mao's thought flourished because of the successes of the Party under Mao's leadership. Yet, as Parris Chang has observed, 'Mao significantly influenced policy but he did not dictate it. Other Party leaders [for example Liu Shaoqi, Zhou Enlai and Deng Xiaoping] were frequently able to block his policies or modify their substance, and the Chairman frequently had to compromise with his colleagues.'[4]

In 1956, however, Mao forced through his vision of socialist development based on the policies of the Great Leap Forward, against the wishes of other Party leaders. Following this débâcle, and his second fall from grace in 1959, Mao was left free to concentrate on ideology, leaving the day-to-day running of government to the more pragmatic Party leaders – dividing Party responsibilities between the 'first line' bureaucratic leaders and the 'second line' theoretical leaders. The principle of the Party as the collective entity of all authority and truth is one of the keystones of Marxism-Leninism, and by setting himself above the Party as the sole arbiter of theory, Mao set a precedent which led directly to the Cultural Revolution.

The Great Leap revealed that Mao's theories had lost their infallibility, and consequently he was forced to legitimize his position as leader of the Party by promoting his own thought, against the pragmatism of Liu, Zhou and Deng, as a universal doctrine in itself. This culminated in 1968 in the Draft Party Constitution, where the concept of *chung*, or absolute loyalty to the ruler, re-emerged as the hallmark of the new proletarian revolutionary. Although the cardinal aim of the Cultural Revolution may have been to eliminate bureaucratism, the methods used in practice drank at the springs of the feudal concept of loyalty.

As Wang Ruoshui, the former deputy editor of the *People's Daily*, argued in a speech in 1979:

The personality cult has deep historical roots in our society. Our country has been primarily dominated by small producers. The small producers' force of habit is very deep-rooted. Patriarchal behaviour and the practice of 'what I say is what counts' is still a very serious problem among the rural cadres. Marx in his work *The Eighteenth Brumaire* . . . made the following analysis of the small farmers. Due to their dispersed, self-sufficient and mutually isolated nature, they were unable to form a 'national bond'. As a result, they cannot represent themselves, they must be represented. Their representative must . . . appear as their master, as an authority over them, as an unlimited governmental power that protects them against the other classes and sends them rain and sunshine from above. This kind of socio-economic condition nurtures monarchical thinking and produces the personality cult.[5]

Even after Mao's death this trait of 'Emperor-ism' continued to play an important part in the development of Chinese Communism. Deng Xiaoping was boxed into the corner of having to criticize Hua Guofeng and his 'whateverist' clique for their 'blind obedience' to Mao Zedong Thought, while at the same time legitimizing his own authority by exalting one important part of Mao's thought, namely that 'practice is the sole criterion of thought'.[6]

Similarly, in reassessing Mao Zedong's achievements, Deng has consistently taken a balanced view. 'In our appraisal of Comrade Mao Zedong we should regard his contributions as primary and his mistakes as secondary,' Deng stated firmly in his speech *Implement the Policy of Readjustment, Ensure Stability and Unity* in 1980. 'To exaggerate under the sway of emotion Comrade Mao's mistakes can only mar the image of our Party and country, impair the prestige of the Party and the socialist system and undermine the unity of the Party, the army and our people of all nationalities.'[7]

The basis of Deng's argument is certainly Leninist, in that the Party is always the ultimate arbiter of theory, but the particular emphasis he gives to a balanced assessment of Mao flows from within the psyche of Chineseness – in that the legitimacy of the Party to continue in power rests with its continuation of a dynastic line. Even the October 1968 Plenum, which condemned Liu Shaoqi as a traitor and expelled him from the Party, was judged constitutional, because, according to Deng, 'To deny their [the Plenum's] legitimacy would pull the rug out from under us.'[8] By staunchly pretending that the Party had not lost control during the Cultural Revolution, and had continued to be the only source of authority, the Dengist argument proceeds that it was only thanks to the Communist Party, using Mao Zedong Thought, that the Gang of Four were defeated.

In refusing to sully the aura of infallibility of Chairman Mao, however, the leaders since 1978 confront an ideological vacuum which they have been singularly unsuccessful in filling. The legitimacy of the Party leaders of the 1980s, and of the Party itself, continued to derive from their struggles against imperialism and the Guomindang before 1949. Indeed, the Communist Party in one sense displays many of the features of the post-1927 Guomindang Party which, having lost its revolutionary telos, took loyalty as the only criterion for admission and adopted an ideology based on conformity and adherence to the dictates of the Party leader, Jiang Jieshi.

But Mao's legitimacy rested not only on the success of his pre-1949 policies, but also on the manner in which he created a unity out of the two opposing contradictions, Chineseness and Communism. By selecting those parts of the Chinese tradition which would serve the ultimate aims of the Chinese Communists, Mao was able to promote a new ideology. One example can be seen in his poetry, where he idealizes the romanticism of Chinese history. In the winter of 1961–2, when China suffered badly from food shortages and was cut off from Soviet aid, Mao wrote a poem using previous crises in Chinese history to show how the new China would eventually overcome its difficulties:

> Above Mount Jiu-i white clouds
> are flying.
> Borne by the wind, the daughters of
> Emperor Yao drift down from the
> blue-green hills.
> Each branch of dappled bamboo has
> been sprinkled with a thousand tears,
> Innumerable rose-coloured clouds
> cover the slopes with manifold
> garments.
> The waves on Lake Dongting boil up
> like snow reaching to the heavens,
> The people of Long Island sing
> earth-shaking songs.
> Inspired by all this, I would dream a
> dream equally vast,
> And see the Land of the Hibiscus
> wholly illuminated by the light
> of dawn.

The beauty of the dappled bamboo came from the tears of Emperor Yao's daughters, who wept on the banks of the Xiang river when their husband, Emperor Shun, died near Mount Jiu-i. Mao looked to the revolutionary experiences of his youth in Long Island, in his native province of Hunan, as the inspiration for his 'dream' of a Land of Hibiscus (the literary name, taken from a T'ang poem, for Hunan) becoming a Communist paradise ('illuminated by the light of dawn').[9]

The leaders after Mao could not offer a comparable ideological legitimacy for the Party, because they could not blend the two contradictory elements into a coherent and practical theory to suit China's needs for the 1970s and 1980s. Indeed, by continuing to work within the confines of Marxist-Leninist-Mao

Zedong Thought, Deng Xiaoping, Hu Yaobang and Zhao Ziyang all cramped their scope for developing the theory. As Zhang Xianliang writes in his *Half of Man is Woman* (from the perspective of an intellectual who was stigmatized for over twenty years after the 1957 Anti-Rightist Campaign),

> Our minds have no time for new creations now, they're totally preoccupied with words. Even if we want to develop in new directions, in these suffocating times we first have to fight our way out with words. It's proof that our 'theory' is nearing a final stage. The final curtain will be when it has led us all the way to the end of the cul-de-sac.[10]

The 'Emperor-ism' of which Mao had taken advantage during the Cultural Revolution is still emphasized with a continuing veneration for the leader, as can be seen in the ongoing dominance of Deng Xiaoping over Party policy direction. While the ideals of collective leadership were stressed in the 1980s, Deng's ultimate authority, like Mao's before him, carried more weight than others when fundamental policy decisions were called for. When Hu Yaobang attempted to introduce the idea of a younger Third Echelon of leaders, who would rule the country while the First Echelon (the pre-1949 'heroes') would 'enjoy long life and quiet dignity' (in retirement) and the Second Echelon (Hu Yaobang's own generation) would 'aid and support the later generations', he came up against the Party conservatives. His dismissal, in January 1987, was both illegal (because he was ousted by an enlarged Politburo meeting) and indicative of the inability of the First Echelon to relinquish the reins of power.

Similarly, during the 1989 Tiananmen Square crisis, Zhao's dismissal was a breach of the rules of the Party Constitution. It also reflected the re-emergence of the pre-1949 revolutionaries, the 'old men', before the footlights of the Chinese political stage, after Hu had vainly tried to banish them to the wings. Zhao's remark to President Gorbachev during the May 1989 demonstrations, that Deng was still in charge, confirmed the survival of 'Emperor-ism' within the Party – as did Deng's official biography in 1984, which described him as 'the most authoritative leader of the Chinese Communist Party at the present time', and Zhao's praises of Deng at that time, which stopped just short of 'Deng Xiaoping Thought', but eerily echoed Liu's eulogy of Mao in 1945.

One explanation for this tendency lies in the two central aims of Chinese Communist theory, to rid the country of imperialism and create a new socialist nation. The legitimacy of these aims rests with the Party representing resistance to imperialism in China. The undeniable experience of the First Echelon of Party leaders gives them authority regarding the evils of imperialism, and their struggle against imperialism, in China. Deng's main supporters during the 1989 crisis were Yang Shangkun, Chen Yun, Li Xiannian, Peng Zhen, Wang Zhen and Deng Yingchao, all of whom have revolutionary credentials from the pre-1949 era.

For the new generation of leaders, legitimacy cannot be based on their leadership capabilities before 1949, and because of this they are obliged to follow the dictates of their more revolutionary elder comrades. Both Hu Yaobang and Zhao Ziyang belonged to the Party when it was following Mao's lines and committed the 'mistakes' of the Great Leap Forward and the Cultural Revolution. Their authority, therefore, rested not on that post-1949 involvement with the Party, but on the consent of the pre-1949 veterans, and, especially, for Hu Yaobang and Zhao Ziyang, on their ties with Deng Xiaoping. The lack of ideological legitimacy was their downfall.

In terms of Chinese tradition, the Party's sustained claim to authority may be viewed as an attempt to consolidate the 'dynastic' succession to the mantle of the Son of Heaven. Looked at from the perspective of Marxism-Leninism, however, all of the changes in the leadership can be explained in terms of the pre-eminent role of the Party. As Deng stated in 1958, 'The key issue is that there is only one Party. If you hold firm on this item, then though you make ten thousand mistakes, you are basically correct. This principle will always be true, right down to the time of the withering of the Party . . .'[11]

While the Party maintains a pre-eminent role, in the best of Marxist-Leninist traditions, its system of decision-making and its ideological legitimation for policy-making ensure that 'Emperor-ism' continues to be a significant feature of Chinese Communism. This contradiction, and the contradictions involved within all spheres of policy-making, mean that the Party has not been able to wean Chinese Communism away from its dependence on the doctrine formulated as a response to Western imperialism. The use of contradictions, moreover, has resulted in Chinese Communism's evolution in a disconcertingly zig-zag manner along its chosen road to the shadowy and distant goal of socialism.

With its tacit acceptance of 'capitalist' methods of development, the Party has recognized the nature of imperialism in the 1990s as fundamentally different from the foreign encroachments on Chinese territory during the nineteenth and early twentieth centuries. Economic imperialism has also altered, and indigenous economic power now proliferates in all corners of Asia. In a sense, Chinese Communist theory now rests on international forces, be they European, Japanese, American or Russian, which no longer exist.

Certainly, Chinese Communism has been successful in lifting China up to a position of some equality and respect in the international community, and in challenging the Eurocentric schools of economic modernization – be they capitalist or communist. It already appears to have been more successful than the 'European' version of Marxism-Leninism.

In terms of national development, however, the effectiveness of Chinese Communism is less easy to measure. It succeeded in increasing the confidence of the Chinese people, bettering the status of women, holding back population growth, in a development challenge infinitely more taxing, because of the numbers, distances and physical handicaps, than any other nation's. Yet, for all their progressive ideas and promise, the Chinese Communists have failed to ensure that steady sustained implementation of theory on which any substantial lasting social change must depend. It would be wise, however, when talking about revolutionary achievements, to bear in mind Mao's remark about whether he thought the French Revolution had been a success – 'it is too early to say', he replied.

In the meantime Chinese Communism is an unfinished agenda, whose consequential social changes appear to have created hopes of some impact in the future. It would be fair to say that in 1949 Chinese Communism offered a model of development towards a more equitable society, but after forty years of national government the Party has been unable to live up to those expectations. After the events of 1989, moreover, the Party faces its most serious test of legitimacy, and will have to become more ideologically flexible if it is to retain the reins of authority.

The theory has foundered on the rivalry and mistrust of individual Party leaders, on the lack of a political machinery to retire the veterans and bring in the fresh perceptions and energies of the young, and on an unwillingness to surrender the ground of chauvinistic nationalism to an as yet unconsolidated universal ideology. The over-arching contradiction between Chineseness and Communism appears to be finding its unity in politics that are recognizably more Chinese than Communist.

But that new Chineseness will not be the old Chineseness of Confucianism or Kang Yuwei or Sun Yat-sen – or even Mao Zedong. It will have been transmuted in the fire of Maoism to reveal new characteristics more appropriate to the time. The tight familial bonds of the neo-Confucianists have slackened, and the social scope of individualism has widened. Only the age-old deference to authority and the predisposition to allow even opponents to preserve their self-respect ('face'), appear to be taking a longer time to change. How the next generation of leaders after Deng Xiaoping will resolve these contradictions will depend on the course and speed of these social adjustments. We may not see the true impact of Chinese Communism until well into the twenty-first century.

Selected Bibliography

Ash, Robert – 'The Evolution of Agricultural Policy' (*China Quarterly*, September 1988)

Bonavia, David – *Deng* (Hong Kong: Longman, 1989)

Burns, John P. – 'China's Governance: Political Reform in a Turbulent Environment' (*China Quarterly*, September 1989)

Chang Pao-min – *The Sino–Vietnamese Territorial Dispute* (The Washington Papers, Center for Strategic & International Studies, 1986)

Cheng, Joseph Y.S. – *China: Modernisation in the 1980s* (Hong Kong: Chinese University Press, 1989)

Daubier, Jean – *A History of the Chinese Cultural Revolution* (New York: Vintage, 1974)

Deng Xiaoping – *Selected Works* (Beijing: Foreign Languages Press, 1984)

Esherick, Joseph W. (ed.) – *Lost Chance in China: The World War II despatches of John S. Service* (New York: Vintage Books, 1975)

Floyd, David – *Mao Against Khrushchev: A Short History of the Sino–Soviet Conflict* (Praeger University Press, 1964)

Gittings, John – *China Changes Face: The Road from Revolution, 1949–1989* (New York: Oxford University Press, 1990)

Goodman, David – *Deng Xiaoping* (London: Cardinal, 1990)

Hao Yufan and Zhai Zhihai – 'China's Decision to Enter the Korean War: History Revisited' (*China Quarterly*, March 1990)

Hicks, George (ed.) – *The Broken Mirror: China after Tiananmen* (London: Longman, 1990)

Hinton, Harold C. – *China's Turbulent Quest: An Analysis of China's Foreign Relations since 1949* (Bloomington and London: Indiana University Press, 1972)

Hou Wai-lu – *A Short History of Chinese Philosophy* (Beijing: Foreign Languages Press, 1959)

Kim, Samuel S. – *China, the United Nations and World Order* (Princeton University Press, 1979)

Kueh, Y.K. – 'The Maoist Legacy and China's New Industrialisation Strategy' (*China Quarterly*, September 1989)

Mao Zedong – *Selected Works*, Volumes I, II, III and IV (Beijing: Foreign Languages Press, 1965 and 1967)

Quested, R.K.I – 'Sino–Russian Relations: A Short History' (London: George Allen & Unwin, 1984)

Schram, Stuart – *Mao Tse-tung* (London: Pelican, 1966) *The Political Thought of Mao Tse-tung*

(New York: Frederick A. Praeger, 1969)

—*Chairman Mao Talks to the People: Talks and Letters, 1956–1971* (New York: Pantheon Books, 1974)

—'China After the 13th Congress' (*China Quarterly*, June 1988)

Schurmann, Franz – *Ideology and Organisation in Communist China* (University of California Press, 1966)

Snow, Edgar – *Red Star Over China* (London: Victor Gollancz, 1937)

Snow, Philip – *The Star Raft: China's Encounter with Africa* (London: Weidenfeld & Nicolson, 1988)

Solomon, Richard H. – *Mao's Revolution and the Chinese Political Culture* (University of California Press, 1971)

Ting Wang – *Chairman Hua: Leader of the Chinese Communists* (London: C. Hurst & Company, 1980)

Wilson, Dick – *China's Revolutionary War* (London: Weidenfeld & Nicolson, 1991)

Yahuda, Michael – 'The People's Republic of China at 40: Foreign Relations' (*China Quarterly*, September 1989)

Yang Zhongmei – *Hu Yaobang: A Chinese Biography* (New York: M.E. Sharpe, 1988)

Zhang Xianliang – *Half of Man is Woman* (London: Penguin, 1988)

Zhao Wei – *The Biography of Zhao Ziyang* (Hong Kong: Educational and Cultural Press Ltd, 1989)

Notes

Mao Zedong – all references to his Selected Works have been abbreviated to 'SW'. These refer, with the exception of SW V, to the four volumes published in Beijing in 1965. SW V was published after Mao's death, in 1977.

All of Mao's works quoted from have been listed within the footnotes. For the sake of space, the *Report on an Investigation of the Peasant Movement in Hunan* (1927) has been shortened to *Hunan Report* after its initial citation. We have also included the date of each work in its initial citation.

Stuart Schram – many of the Mao quotes have been taken from Schram's works, the main three being *Mao Tse-tung, The Political Thought of Mao Tse-tung*, and *Chairman Mao Talks to the People*. These have been shortened to Schram, *Mao*, Schram, *Political* and Schram, *Chairman*.

For the following authors – John Gittings, Yang Zhongmei, Franz Schurmann and Richard Solomon – their works have been cited only where they first appear in the footnotes, otherwise they appear as, e.g. Gittings, *op. cit.*

The *Foreign Relations of the United States* has also been shortened to *FRUS* after its first citation.

1 Introduction (pp. 1–18)

1 Mao Zedong, *The Chinese Revolution and the Chinese Communist Party*, December 1939; SW II, p. 313.

2 C.M. Lewis, 'The Hunanese Elite and the Reform Movement, 1895–1898', in *Journal of Asian Studies*, 1969–70. Hunan province, whose sons and daughters later played such a crucial part in the Chinese Communist Party, was the centre of the Self-Strengthening Movement, especially through the actions of the Governor, Zhang Zhidong and the leading intellectual, Jiang Biao.

3 Mao also used *Datong* – see Chapter 4. Another similarity Kang shared with Mao was his emphasis on the importance of self-criticism. After the German landing at Jiaozhou Bay in 1897, during the foreign 'scramble for concessions', Kang asked the Emperor to blame himself, so that his self-criticism would unite the people behind the throne.

4 Hou Wai-lu, *A Short History of Chinese Philosophy* (Beijing: Foreign Languages Press, 1959), p. 102.

5 *Ibid.*, p. 112.

6 Mao Zedong, *On New*

Democracy, January 1940; SW II, p. 374.

7 Hou Wai-lu, *op. cit.*, p. 93.

8 Stuart Schram, *The Political Thought of Mao Tse-tung* (New York: Praeger, 1969), p. 32.

9 *Ibid.*, p. 44.

10 Mao Zedong, *Report on an Investigation of the Peasant Movement in Hunan*, March 1927; SW I, p. 23.

11 Mao Zedong, *On the New Stage*, report to the Sixth Plenum of the Sixth Central Committee, October 1938, in Schram, *op. cit.*, pp. 172–3.

12 *Ibid.*, p. 171.

13 Franz Schurmann, *Ideology and Organisation in Communist China* (Los Angeles: University of California Press, 1966), p. 26.

14 *Ibid.*, p. 28.

15 Mao Zedong, *On Practice*, July 1937; SW I, p. 300.

16 Yang Zhongmei, *Hu Yaobang, A Chinese Biography* (London: M.E. Sharpe, 1988), p. 130. Hua Guofeng's 'Two Whatevers' were, 'We will resolutely uphold whatever policy decisions Chairman Mao made, and unswervingly follow whatever instructions Chairman Mao gave.'

17 Yang, *op. cit.*, p. 131.

18 John Gittings, *China Changes Face: The Road from Revolution, 1949–1989* (New York: OUP, 1990), p. 206.

19 Yang, *op. cit.*, pp. 169–71. In 1983 a *Red Flag* article attributed the origin of the phrase, 'seek truth from facts', to a speech given by Mao Zedong during the 1943 Rectification Campaign – 'discover the truth through practice,' Mao stated, 'and again through practice verify the truth.'

20 Su was later sacked from his position at the Institute.

21 Mao Zedong, *On Contradiction*, August 1937; SW I, p. 345.

22 Schram, *op. cit.*, p. 92.

23 Yang, *op. cit.*, p. 172.

24 *Ibid.*, pp. 173–4.

25 Mao Zedong, *Talks on Questions of Philosophy*, in Stuart Schram, *Chairman Mao Talks to the People* (New York: Pantheon, 1974), p. 226.

26 Mao Zedong, *On Contradictions*, SW I, p. 333.

27 Yang, *op. cit.*, p. 174.

28 *Ibid.*, p. 175.

29 Mao Zedong, *Talks at Chengdu; Talk of 20 March*, in Schram, *Chairman*, p. 108.

30 Mao Zedong, *Speech at the Supreme State Conference*, January 1958, in Schram, *Chairman*, p. 94.

31 Schurmann, *op. cit.*, p. 26.

32 Gittings, *op. cit.*, p. 256.

33 Zhao Ziyang, 'Advance Along the Road of Socialism with Chinese Characteristics', 1987, *Beijing Review*, Number 45.

34 Gittings, *op. cit.*, pp. 41–2.

35 *Ibid.*, p. 208.

36 Joseph Y.S. Cheng, 'China's Post-Tiananmen Diplomacy', in George Hicks (ed.), *The Broken Mirror: China after Tiananmen* (London: Longman, 1990), p. 412.

37 Mao Zedong, *Never Forget Class Struggle*, speech at Tenth Plenum of Chinese Communist Party, in Gittings, *op. cit.*, p. 41.

2 Democracy vs. Centralism (pp. 19–42)

1 Richard H. Solomon, *Mao's Revolution and the Chinese Political Culture* (University of California Press, 1971), pp. 164–5.

2 Chang Kuo-t'ao, *The Rise of the Chinese Communist Party, 1921–1927*, Volume I (University Press of Kansas, 1971), p. 309.

3 For a military account of the Chinese Communist Revolution, see Dick Wilson, *China's Revolutionary War* (London: Weidenfeld, 1991).

4 Mao Zedong, *Hunan Report*, SW I, pp. 23–4.

5 Mao Zedong, *Analysis of the Classes in Chinese Society*, SW I, p. 18.

6 Mao Zedong, *Hunan Report*, SW I, p. 27.

7 Mao Zedong, *The Force of the Peasantry and the Leadership of the Workers*, April 1929; quoted in Schram, *Political*, p. 260.

8 Mao Zedong, *A Single Spark can start a Prairie Fire*, January 1930, SW I, pp. 118–19.

9 Mao Zedong, *The Chinese Revolution and the Chinese Communist Party*, December 1939, SW II, pp. 324–5.

10 Mao Zedong, *On New Democracy*, January 1940, SW II, p. 348.

11 *Ibid.*, pp. 348–9.

12 *Ibid.*, pp. 341–2.

13 Mao Zedong, *On the People's Democratic Dictatorship*, June 1949, SW IV, p. 421. Mao continued to acknowledge that 'the Chinese revolution is in essence a revolution of the peasantry', but that 'without the workers the [Chinese] revolution would not succeed'.

14 Mao Zedong, *On New Democracy*, SW II, p. 352.

15 Mao Zedong, *On the People's Democratic Dictatorship*, SW IV, p. 420.

16 Mao Zedong, *Report to Second Session of Seventh Central Committee*, March 1949, SW IV, p. 372.

17 Stuart Schram, *Mao Zedong: A Preliminary Reassessment* (Hong Kong: Chinese University Press, 1973), p. 41.

18 Stuart Schram, *Chairman*, p. 11.

19 Mao Zedong, *On Correcting Mistaken Ideas in the Party*, December 1929, SW I, p. 109.

20 Mao Zedong, *Rectify the Party's Style of Work*, February 1942, SW III, p. 44.

21 Mao Zedong, *Report to Second Session*, SW IV, p. 363. Mao stressed, however, that 'under no circumstances should the village be ignored and only the city given attention'.

22 Others included the All-China Association of Literary Workers, the All-China Association of Cinema Workers and the All-China Association of Fine Art Workers.

23 Schurmann, *op. cit.*, p. xxxiii.

24 Gittings, *op. cit.*, p. 49.

25 Mao Zedong, *Some Questions Concerning Methods of Leadership*, June 1943, SW III, p. 119.

26 Schurmann, *op. cit.*, p. 87.

27 Schram, *Chairman*, p. 13.

28 Mao Zedong, *On the Correct Handling of Contradictions*

Among the People, June 1957, in Yang, op. cit., p. 97.

29 Mao Zedong, *Speech at the 7,000 Cadres Conference*, January 1972, in Schram, *Chairman.*, p. 163.

30 Mao Zedong, *On the Correct Handling*, SW V, p. 385.

31 Gittings, op. cit., p. 208.

32 Ibid., p. 76.

33 Ibid., p. 77.

34 Mao Zedong, *Problems of War and Strategy*, November 1937, SW II, p. 224.

35 Mao Zedong, *Talk at the First Plenum of the Ninth Central Committee of the Chinese Communist Party*, April 1969, in Schram, op. cit., p. 288.

36 Mao Zedong, *Stalin is our Commander*, in Schram, *Political Thought of Mao Tse-tung*, pp. 427–8.

37 Mao Zedong, *Speech at the 7,000 Cadres Conference*, in Schram, *Chairman*, p. 187.

38 John P. Burns, 'China's Governance: Political Reform in a Turbulent Environment', in *China Quarterly*, September 1989, p. 512.

39 Joseph Y.S. Cheng, 'Whither China's Reforms', in

Joseph Cheng (ed.), *China: Modernization in the 1980s* (Hong Kong: Chinese University Press, 1989), p. 664.

40 Stuart Schram, 'China After the Thirteenth Congress', in *China Quarterly*, June 1988, p. 182.

41 Yang, op. cit., p. 159.

42 Central Committee of the Chinese Communist Party, 7 February 1990.

43 Deng Xiaoping, *People's Daily*, 28 December 1989.

44 Gittings, op. cit., p. 262.

45 Burns, op. cit., p. 501.

46 *China Quarterly*, Chronicle and Documentation, March 1990, p. 170.

47 Jiang Zemin, speech at Fifth Plenary Session of Thirteenth Central Committee of Chinese Communist Party, 9 November 1989.

48 Gittings, op. cit., p. 193.

49 Burns, op. cit., pp. 490–91.

50 Ibid., p. 494.

51 Ibid., p. 514.

52 Yang, op. cit., p. 158.

53 Liao Gailong, *Report*, in Bill Brugger, 'Ideology, Legitimacy and Marxist Theory', in Cheng (ed.), *China: Modernization in the 1980s*, p. 9.

3 State vs. Market (pp. 43–65)

1 Bruce Chatwin, *What Am I Doing Here?* (London: Picador, 1989), p. 197.

2 Mao Zedong, *On the People's Democratic Dictatorship*, SW IV, p. 422.

3 From 1937 to 1949 Chinese inflation is estimated at 151.6×10^{12}. The German inflationary spiral after the First World War was estimated at $1.26 \times$

10^{12}. See Chang Kiang-gua, *The Inflationary Spiral: The Experience of China, 1939–50* p. 314.

4 Mao Zedong, *Report to Second Session of Seventh Central Committee*, March 1949, SW IV, p. 369.

5 C. Brandt, B. Schwartz and J.K. Fairbank, *A Documentary History of Chinese*

Communism (New York: 1952), p. 444.

6 Mao Zedong, *On New Democracy*, SW II, p. 353.

7 New China News Agency, 25 October 1949.

8 New China News Agency, 12 May 1950.

9 New China News Agency, 29 November 1949.

10 New China News Agency, 22 November 1949.

11 The Basic Agrarian Law, 10 October 1947, was based on four principles: i) Land to the tiller on the basis of equal distribution to men and women/young and old, with the *xiang* (village administration unit) as the normal unit of distribution; ii) Peasant associations in charge of confiscation and redistribution under Communist Party direction; iii) All land of landlords and surplus of rich peasants to be confiscated; iv) Land following distribution to be freely bought and sold and, with certain restrictions, rented.

12 New China News Agency, 2 May 1950, announced the establishment of the first model state farm at Gaoli, north east of Tianjin, based on the Soviet crop-rotation theories of Michurin.

13 Mao Zedong, *On the People's Democratic Dictatorship*, SW IV, p. 422. ·

14 *Ibid.*, p. 417.

15 Gittings, op. cit., p. 15.

16 Mao Zedong, *Speech at the Supreme State Conference*, January 1958, in Schram, *Chairman*, p. 93.

17 Stuart Schram, *Mao Tse-tung* (Pelican, 1966), p. 261.

18 According to Bill Brugger, this attempt to instil the theory of 'uninterrupted revolution' into economic theory turned Chinese 'socialism into something which resembled more a Weberian ideal-type than anything Marxian'. Brugger, 'Ideology, Legitimacy and Marxist Theory', in Cheng (ed.), *China: Modernization in the 1980s*, pp. 4–5.

19 Schurmann, *op. cit.*, p. xiii.

20 Mao Zedong, *On the Ten Great Relationships*, April 1956, in Schram, *Chairman*, p. 65.

21 Schurmann, *op. cit.*, p. 82, fn. 55.

22 Schram, *Mao*, pp. 280–81.

23 Schurmann, *op. cit.*, p. 81.

24 Schram, *Mao*, p. 295.

25 Mao Zedong, *Speech at the Supreme State Conference*, in Schram, *Chairman*, p. 33.

26 Schram, *Mao*, pp. 292–3. Schram calls this a striking example of Mao's 'military romanticism'.

27 Alan Winnington, *Breakfast with Mao* (London: Lawrence & Wishart, 1986), p. 248.

28 Dick Wilson, *Anatomy of China* (London: Mentor, 1969), p. 29.

29 Mao Zedong, *People's Daily*, January 1967, in Dick Wilson, 'China's Economic Situation', in *Bulletin of the Atomic Scientists*, November 1967.

30 Schram, *Mao*, p. 277.

31 Dick Wilson, *New Nation*, 19 January 1977.

32 Mao Zedong, *Speech at 7,000 Cadres Conference*, in Schram, *Chairman*, p. 178.

33 Schram, *Chairman*, p. 32.

34 Gittings, *op. cit.*, pp. 105–6.

35 Mao Zedong, *Talk to Music Workers*, August

1956, in Schram, *Chairman*, pp. 85–6.

36 Mao Zedong, *Speech at Hangzhou*, December 1965, in Schram, *Chairman*, p. 235.

37 Yang, *op. cit.*, p. 136.

38 *Daily Telegraph*, 1 October 1990.

39 Zhao Ziyang, 1987 Party Report, as quoted in Gittings, *op. cit.*, p. 234.

40 Gittings, *op. cit.*, p. 235.

41 Schurmann, *op. cit.*, p. 76.

42 Gittings, *op. cit.*, p. 115.

43 *Resolution on Certain Questions of Party History*, in *ibid.*, p. 115.

44 Robert Ash, 'The Evolution of Agricultural Policy', in *China Quarterly*, September 1988.

45 *People's Daily*, 4 February 1982, in Ash, *op. cit.*, p. 535.

46 *China Quarterly*, Chronicles and Documentation, March 1990, pp. 172–3.

47 Gittings, *op. cit.*, p. 142.

48 Li Peng, 4 August 1990, *Inside China Mainland*, October 1990.

49 Bill Brugger, *op. cit.*, in Cheng (ed.), *China*, p. 5.

50 Gittings, *op. cit.*, p. 109.

51 *Ibid.*, p. 258.

4 Red vs. Expert (pp. 66–88)

1 Gittings, *China*, p. 87.

2 In 1967 Mao personally disavowed his label of 'The Four Greats', after the successful testing of the Chinese H-bomb had been attributed to his thought. A year later he forbade anyone to refer to 'inculcating the absolute authority' of his thought. See Jean Daubier, *A History of the Chinese Cultural Revolution* (New York: Vintage, 1974), pp. 263–4.

3 Mao Zedong, *Hunan Report*, SW I, p. 44.

4 Mao Zedong, *Report to the Central Committee*, November 1928, in Schram, *Political*, p. 269.

5 Mao Zedong, *Oppose Bookism*, May 1930, in Dick Wilson, *Mao: The People's Emperor* (London: Hutchinson, 1979), p. 143.

6 *Ibid.*, pp. 143–4.

7 Mao Zedong, *On New Democracy*, SW II, pp. 372–3.

8 *Ibid.*, pp. 380–81.

9 Mao Zedong, *Rectify the Party's Style of Work*, February 1942, SW III, pp. 41–2.

10 According to Stuart Schram, 'Mao tends to exalt the revolutionary will of human beings until it becomes not merely an important factor in history, but an all-powerful force capable of reshaping the material environment in a completely arbitrary fashion' (Schram, *Political*, p. 79).

11 Mao stated that, 'But for the working class, the labouring people, and the Communist Party, the question is not one of being overthrown, but of working hard to create the conditions in which classes, state power, and political parties will die out very naturally and mankind will enter the realm of Great Harmony (*Datong*).' *Datong* was a traditional term used by the fourth-century B.C. philosopher, Mozi. See Gittings, *ibid.*, p. 19.

12 Richard Solomon, *Mao's Revolution*, p. 153. Confucius's *Book of Rites* states that, 'When the Great Way prevailed in the world, all mankind worked

for the common good. Men of virtue and ability were elected to fill public offices. Good faith was universally observed and friendly relations cultivated . . . The people were loath to let the natural resources lie undeveloped in the earth; but they did not desire to hoard riches in their own houses. They were ashamed to be idle; but they did not labour for their own profit. In this way, the source of all greed was stopped up, and there was no occasion for the rise of theft and banditry, nor was there any need to lock the outer door of one's house. This is called the Age of Grand Harmony (*Datong*).' See John C.H. Wu, 'Chinese Legal and Political Philosophy', in Charles A. Moore (ed.), *The Chinese Mind: Essentials of Chinese Philosophy and Culture* (University Press of Hawaii, 1977), p. 229.

13 Mao Zedong, *Hunan Report*, SW I, p. 47.

14 *Ibid.*, p. 37.

15 Schram, *Mao*, pp. 260–61.

16 Mao Zedong, *Rectify the Party's Style of Work*, SW III, p. 38.

17 Schurmann, *op. cit.*, p. 93.

18 *Ibid.*, p. 92.

19 Mao Zedong, *On the Correct Handling of Contradictions Among the People*, in Schurmann, *op. cit.*, p. 75.

20 Mao, quoted in Schram, *Mao*, p. 288.

21 Deng Xiaoping, quoted in Yang, *op. cit.*, p. 114. The 'Hot Pepper' supplements (*fukan*), with a spirit of 'making revolution in every issue', printed a number of sharp, biting attacks on bureaucratism and exposing social evils. Among those contributing were Liu Binyan, who continues to attack bureaucratism and nepotism within the government. See Yang, *ibid.*, p. 95.

22 Mao, quoted in Schram, *Mao*, p. 289.

23 Gittings, *op. cit.*, p. 71. Hu Yaobang revealed in 1983 that, 'In 1957, I had a talk with Lin Xiling for four hours. She wouldn't listen to me, but I never thought she should be arrested.' Hu pointed out to her that 'her thinking was dominated by the ideology of individualism, and that there was no future in this kind of approach.' See Yang, *op. cit.*, p. 97.

24 Mao Zedong, *On the Ten Great Relationships*, April 1956, in Schram, *Chairman*, p. 78.

25 Mao, quoted in Schram, *Mao*, p. 292.

26 One team cadre explained the problems of implementing the work points system. 'I have tried the system of assigning work points to quotas. I spent a lot of energy making different rules for how many work points there should be if one does this kind or that kind of work and if one performs a certain amount of work. In the case of ploughing, for instance, the rules for work points differed depending on whether one used a strong or weak buffalo, or one of average strength. Even for the same kind of buffalo, there were also different kinds of land, and for the same type of land, the case was also different if it rained or if the soil was dry . . . With so many rules, it was almost endless. If they were printed in

a book, it would be quite a thick edition. They were so elaborate the peasants were not interested at all' (Gittings, *op. cit.*, p. 135).

27 Karl Marx, *Das Kapital*, quoted in Yang, *op. cit.*, p. 181.

28 Schram, *Chairman*, p. 29.

29 Mao Zedong, *Remarks at the Spring Festival*, February 1964, in "Schram, *Chairman*, p. 210.

30 Mao Zedong, *Talks with Mao Yuanxin*, first talk, July 1964, in Schram, *Chairman*, p. 246.

31 Mao Zedong, *On Khrushchev's Phoney Communism and Its Historical Lessons for the World*, May 1963, in *Quotations from Chairman Mao Tse-tung* (New York: Bantam Books, 1967), p. 22.

32 Yang, *op. cit.*, p. 112. Poems by Mao, Liu Shaoqi, Zhou Enlai and Deng Xiaoping appeared in *China Youth*, praising the late Lei Feng. The Youth League Central Committee issued an 'Announcement on the Educational Activities of Young People Throughout the Nation to Learn from Lei Feng'.

33 Gittings, *op. cit.*, p. 55.

34 Mao Zedong, *Against Blind Faith in Learning*, March 1958, in Schram, *Chairman*, p. 120.

35 Gittings, *op. cit.*, p. 74.

36 Mao Zedong, *Talks with Mao Yuanxin*, third talk, 1966, in Schram, *Chairman*, p. 251.

37 Mao quoted in Schram, *Political*, p. 110.

38 Mao Zedong, *Talks with Mao Yuanxin*, first talk, July 1964, in Schram, *Chairman*, p. 248.

39 Gittings, *op. cit.*, p. 160. One result of the re-education movement was the emergence of the Shengwulian Group, whose pamphlet, *Whither China?* challenged the ultra-leftists within the Party. According to Gittings, this tract 'stands in a classic line of revolutionary challenge which extends from Mao's own early pronouncements through the Beida (Beijing University) protests of the Hundred Flowers to the post-Mao democracy movement' (*ibid.*, p. 81).

40 Schurmann, *op. cit.*, p. 48.

41 Mao Zedong, *Hunan Report*, SW I, p. 28.

42 Mao, quoted in Schram, *Political*, pp. 135–6.

43 Deng, quoted in David Bonavia, *Deng* (Hong Kong: Longman, 1989), pp. 232–3.

44 Yang, *op. cit.*, p. 124.

45 Gittings, *op. cit.*, p. 215.

46 Li Peng, *China Daily*, 15 January 1990; in Jerome Alan Cohen, 'Tiananmen and the Rule of Law', in Hicks (ed.), *Broken Mirror*, p. 329.

47 *Guardian*, 23 September 1990.

48 Gittings, *op. cit.*, p. 151. Wei was sentenced to fifteen years (longer than any of the 'leaders' of the 1989 democracy movement), for his criticisms of the political system, and in particular his attacks on the imperial style of Deng Xiaoping.

49 Gittings, *op. cit.*, p. 212.

50 *Ibid.*, pp. 57–8.

5 Idealism vs. Realpolitik (pp. 89–110)

1 Schram, *Political*, p. 374.
2 Schram, *Mao*, p. 254.
3 *Ibid.*, p. 254.
4 Mao Zedong, *The Chinese Revolution and the Chinese Communist Party*, December 1939, SW II, p. 311.
5 Schram, *Mao*, pp. 282–3.
6 Philip Snow, *The Star Raft: China's Encounter with Africa* (London: Weidenfeld & Nicolson, 1988), pp. 73–4.
7 *Ibid.*, p. 75.
8 Schram, *Mao*, p. 312.
9 Snow, *op. cit.*, p. 86.
10 *Ibid.*, p. 119.
11 *Ibid.*, p. 123.
12 Yang, *op. cit.*, pp. 177–8.
13 Snow, *op. cit.*, p. 186.
14 New China News Agency, 2 November 1951.
15 Mao Zedong, *On the People's Democratic Dictatorship*, SW IV, p. 416.
16 Chang Pao-min, 'The Sino–Vietnamese Territorial Dispute' (*The Washington Papers*, 1986), p. 52. The fighting lasted for seventeen days, with only troops being sent into battle. According to Chang, 'unlike any nation engaged in a military operation of such a scale, Beijing made it clear from the beginning that the Chinese action would be limited in both scope and duration, that China did not want "a single inch" of Vietnamese territory, and that Chinese troops would be withdrawn as soon as they had administered the punishment Vietnam deserved and accomplished their mission' (Chang, p. 55).
17 Chang, *op. cit.*, p. 54.
18 Mao Zedong, *Letter to the Secretary-General of the Indian Communist Party*, in Schram, *Political*, p. 379.
19 Mao Zedong, *Talks with African Visitors*, August 1963, in Schram, *Political*, p. 382.
20 John Pilger, *Heroes* (London: Jonathan Cape, 1989), p. 183. Pilger criticizes Zhou's role in the Indo-China conference at Geneva in 1954, saying that he preferred a divided Vietnam. According to Anthony Barrett, Zhou secretly told the French that 'he recognized the reality of the South Vietnamese government they were trying to create' (*ibid.*, p. 183).
21 Dick Wilson, 'Taking Tips from Horse's Mouth', *Bangkok Post*, 19 November 1975.
22 *Bangkok Post*, 12 January 1975.
23 'Former Rebel Beauty now a Poet', *Japan Times*, 22 September 1989.
24 See Dick Wilson, *Hongkong! Hongkong!* (London: Unwin Hyman, 1991).
25 Michael Yahuda, 'The People's Republic of China at 40: Foreign Relations', in *China Quarterly*, September 1989, p. 531.
26 In July 1989, Foreign Minister Qian Qichen visited six African countries. Li Peng stated in the same month that 'The profound friendship and close co-operation existing between China and Africa can stand the test of storms.' See, for example, *Japan Times*, 27 July 1989.
27 'Cambodia Discord', *Far Eastern Economic Review*, 20 June 1990.
28 Yang, *op. cit.*, p. 178.

6 Marxism vs. Nationalism (pp. 111–136)

1 Hou Wai-lu, *A Short History of Chinese Philosophy* (Beijing: Foreign Languages Press, 1959), pp. 152–3.

2 According to Chang Guo-tao, 'When this telegram was read at a meeting of the Political Bureau of the CC of the CCP, everyone present had the reaction of not knowing whether to laugh or cry' (Chang Guo-tao, *The Rise of the Chinese Communist Party: 1921–1927 – Volume One*, University Press of Kansas, 1971, p. 637).

3 Bruce Chatwin, *What Am I Doing Here?*, p. 168.

4 Franz Michael, 'China and the Crisis of Communism', in Hicks (ed.), *Broken Mirror*, pp. 447–8.

5 Schram, *Political*, pp. 117–18.

6 Vladimer Dedijer, 'Tito Speaks', as quoted in David Floyd, *Mao Against Khrushchev* (London: Praeger, 1964), p. 211, and W.W. Rostow, *The Prospects for Communist China* (New York: 1954), p. 57.

7 N.B. Tucker, *Patterns in the Dust: Chinese–American Relations and the Recognition Controversy, 1949–1950* (New York: Columbia University Press, 1983), p. 29.

8 Mao Zedong, *On New Democracy*, SW II, p. 364.

9 Mao Zedong, *On the People's Democratic Dictatorship*, SW IV, p. 415.

10 *Foreign Relations of the United States*, 1949, Volume 8, p. 478.

11 D. Beloff, *Soviet Policy in the Far East, 1944–1951* (London: Oxford University Press, 1953), p. 73.

12 *Ibid.*, p. 74.

13 New China News Agency, 9 November 1949.

14 *South China Morning Post*, 14 May 1989. Stalin's intransigence over Soviet conditions led to Zhou's threatening to resign – see *FRUS*, 1949, Volume 8, pp. 294–311.

15 John Gittings, 'The Origins of China's Foreign Policy', in D. Horowitz (ed.), *Containment and Revolution* (Boston: Beacon Press, 1967), pp. 212–13.

16 Tucker, *op. cit.*, p. 225.

17 In 1949 the United States estimated that railway rehabilitation in China alone would cost $300 million in imported machinery and equipment.

18 The Chinese were reportedly angry that the Soviets had bought over 100,000 tonnes of West German steel rails and then sold them to the Chinese at 100 per cent profit. See *FRUS*, Volume 8, 1949, pp. 633–4.

19 According to *FRUS*, 'Tan Gaguo, [the] great industrial patriot, had actually wept on Mao's shoulder in complaining to him of Soviet encroachments especially [in] Manchuria' (*FRUS*, Volume 8, 1949, p. 635).

20 Ironically, the US Navy, through its External Data Unit, had been engaged in espionage activities in Manchuria since 1946. See Tucker, *ibid.*, p. 44.

21 Peng Dehuai, quoted in Hao Yufan and Zhai Zhihai, 'China's Decision to Enter the Korean War: History Revisited', *China Quarterly*, March 1990, p. 106.

22 According to Hao and Zhai, Stalin gave the Chinese more than two hundred jets, with Soviet pilots dressed as Chinese People's Volunteers; weapon equipment for more than sixty army divisions; and 80 per cent of the total ammunition.

23 Schram, *Mao*, pp. 283–4.

24 *Ibid.*, p. 286. In 1963, Mao asked in the *Beijing Review*, 'In what position does Khrushchev, who participated in the leadership of the Party and the state during Stalin's period, place himself when he beats his breast, pounds the table and shows abuse of Stalin at the top of his voice? In the position of an accomplice to a "murderer" or a "bandit"? Or in the same position as a "fool" or an "idiot"?' – *ibid.*, p. 285.

25 *Ibid.*, p. 285.

26 Roy Medvedev, 'China and the Superpowers', in *Far Eastern Economic Review*, 7 April 1988.

27 Floyd, *op. cit.*, p. 34.

28 Schram, *Mao*, p. 290.

29 *Ibid.*, pp. 291–2.

30 Floyd, *op. cit.*, p. 42.

31 *Red Flag*, 'More on the Differences Between Comrade Togliatti and Us . . .', March 1963, in Floyd, *op. cit.*, p. 43.

32 Schram, *Chairman*, p. 83.

33 *Ibid.*, p. 33.

34 Floyd, *op. cit.*, pp. 64–5.

35 *Ibid.*, p. 263. See also Schram, *Mao*, p. 301. Khrushchev went on to allude to Lenin's decision after the 1917 revolution of accepting a 'temporary concession' in the Soviet Far Eastern Republic, in an allusion to the 'Two Chinas' situation.

36 Floyd, *op. cit.*, p. 146.

37 Schram, *Political*, pp. 119–20.

38 Michael Lindsay, 'The Ideology of Chinese Communism', in Hicks (ed.), *Broken Mirror*, p. 215.

39 Floyd, *op. cit.*, p. 410.

40 *The Sunday Times*, 7 February 1988.

41 Mao Zedong, *In Memory of Norman Bethune*, December 1939, SW II, pp. 337–8.

42 In 1964, in response to Soviet requests for business contacts, Mao stated that, 'We can do a little business, but we can't do too much, for Soviet products are heavy, crude, high-priced and they always keep something back.' It was better, therefore, in terms of technology transfer, for the Chinese to deal with the French bourgeoisie, because 'they still have some notion of business ethics'. See Schram, *Chairman*, p. 39.

43 Joseph Y.S. Cheng, 'The Evolution of China's Foreign Policy in the post-Mao era: from anti-hegemony to modernization diplomacy', in Cheng (ed.), *China: Modernization in the 1980s*, p. 198.

44 *Ibid.*, p. 179.

45 Stuart Schram, 'China After the Thirteenth Congress', in *China Quarterly*, June 1988, p. 182.

46 Joseph Y.S. Cheng, 'China's Post-Tiananmen Diplomacy', in Hicks (ed.), *Broken Mirror*, p. 408.

7 Imperialism vs. Pragmatism (pp. 137–58)

1 Samuel S. Kim, *China, the United Nations and World Order* (Princeton University Press, 1979), p. 20.

2 *Ibid.*, p. 29.

3 *Ibid.*, pp. 41–4.

4 Edgar Snow, *Red Star Over China* (London: Left Book Club, 1938), p. 96.

5 See Edgar Snow, *Journey from the Beginning* (New York: Vintage, 1972), p. 26 for Fessenden's role in the Shanghai massacre. See also Sterling Seagrave, *The Soong Dynasty* (New York: Harper & Row, 1985), pp. 221–2.

6 John S. Service, *Lost Chance in China* (New York: Vintage, 1975), p. 292.

7 *Ibid.*, p. 295.

8 *Ibid.*, p. 307.

9 *Ibid.*, pp. 372–3.

10 *Ibid.*, p. 373.

11 Mao Zedong, *Farewell, Leighton Stuart!*, August 1949, SW IV, p. 436.

12 Mao Zedong, *Talk with Anna Louise Strong*, August 1946, SW IV, p. 101.

13 W.W. Rea and J.C. Brener, *The Forgotten Ambassador: The Reports of John Leighton Stuart, 1946–1949* (Boulder: Westview Press, 1981), p. 338.

14 *FRUS*, 1949, Volume 8, p. 626.

15 *FRUS*, 1949, Volume 9, pp. 151–2.

16 Mao Zedong, *Address to the Preparatory Committee of the New Political Consultative Conference*, June 1949, SW IV, p. 408.

17 J.K. Fairbank, *The United States and China* (Massachusetts: Harvard University Press, 1958), pp. 3–4.

18 Tucker, *op. cit.*, p. 35.

19 McCarthy stated in 1950 that 'it was not Chinese democracy under Mao that conquered China, as Acheson, Lattimore, Jessup and Harrison [State Department officials] contend. Soviet Russia conquered China and an important ally of the conquerors was this small left-wing element in our Department of State.'

20 Foreign Office minute – F18695/1023/10, F0371/75826, 5 December 1949.

21 Foreign Office minute – F18695/1023/10, F0371/75826, 15 December 1949. Sixty per cent of the population in Singapore and 40 per cent of the population in Malaysia were Chinese. There were also two million Chinese in Hong Kong.

22 Foreign Office minute – G18848/1023/10, F0371/75827, 16 December 1949.

23 *FRUS*, 1949, Volume 8, p. 203.

24 Tucker, *op. cit.*, p. 55. Acheson was quoted on 10 January 1950 as saying that 'it hurts the fellow who does not recognize it much more than the person who is not recognized. It is of absolutely no use in trying to affect the internal operations of a government.'

25 According to M. Schaller, 'The issue of China became only a means to an end – gaining political power by stoking fears of treason and conspiracy committed by career officials and the Democratic Party', in *The United States and China in*

the Twentieth Century (London: Oxford University Press, 1979), p. 127.

26 Zhou Enlai, 30 September 1950, in Hao and Zhai, *op. cit.*, p. 104.

27 Zhou in *ibid.*, p. 105.

28 *Ibid.*, p. 106.

29 Service, *op. cit.*, p. 193.

30 Kim, *op. cit.*, p. 63.

31 *Ibid.*, pp. 65–6.

32 Schram, *Chairman*, p. 40.

33 Kim, *op. cit.*, p. 71.

34 Schram, *Mao*, p. 131.

35 Kim, *op. cit.*, p. 71.

36 *Ibid.*, p. 68 – see also Schram, *Chairman*, pp. 285–6.

37 Kim, *op. cit.*, p. 130.

38 *Ibid.*, p. 494.

39 *People's Daily*, 'A Comment on the Statement of the Communist Party of the USA', March 1963, in Floyd, *op. cit.*, p. 389.

40 Gittings, *op. cit.*, p. 230.

41 By 1986 China had issued 'the first international bond under communism', worth $50 million and underwritten by a ten-bank international consortium.

42 Gittings, *op. cit.*, p. 228.

43 Hu Yaobang, address to the Twelfth Communist Party Congress, 1982, in Joseph Cheng, 'The Evolution of China's Foreign Policy', in Cheng (ed.), *China: Modernization in the 1980s*, p. 167.

44 *Ibid.*, p. 186.

45 *Ibid.*, p. 162.

46 *Ibid.*, pp. 168–9.

47 Appendix, in Hicks (ed.), *Broken Mirror*, p. 486.

8   Conclusion (pp. 159–68)

1 Liu Shaoqi, *How to be a Good Communist*, in Gittings, *op. cit.*, p. 50.

2 Solomon, *Mao*, p. 6.

3 Mao Zedong, *On the Problem of Stalin*, March 1958, in Schram, *Chairman*, p. 99.

4 Parris Chang, 'Power and Policy in China', in Ting Wang, *Chairman Hua: Leader of the Chinese Communists* (London: C. Hurst, 1980), p. 127.

5 Wang Ruoshui, speech at conference on theoretical work of CCP Central Committee, in Bill Brugger, 'Ideology, Legitimacy and Marxist Theory', in Cheng (ed.), *China: Modernization in the 1980s*, p. 22.

6 Even before Mao's death in 1976, the Chinese media began glorifying Empress Lu (wife of Liu Pang, founder of the Han Dynasty) and Empress Wu Tse-tien (wife of the second emperor of the T'ang Dynasty and the first female ruling monarch in Chinese history), in preparation for Jiang Qing's 'succession' to the throne.

7 Deng Xiaoping, *Implement the Policy of Readjustment, Ensure Stability and Unity*, December 1980, SW I, p. 347.

8 Gittings, *op cit.*, pp. 183–4.

9 Schram, *Mao*, pp. 304–5.

10 Zhang Xianliang, *Half of Man is Woman* (London: Penguin, 1988), pp. 89–90.

11 Deng, quoted in Yang, *op. cit.*, p. 114.

Index